THE
PROSPEROUS HEART

CREATING A LIFE OF "ENOUGH"

Julia Cameron

JEREMY P. TARCHER/PENGUIN
a member of Penguin Group (USA) Inc.
New York

JEREMY P. TARCHER/PENGUIN
Published by the Penguin Group
Penguin Group (USA) Inc., 375 Hudson Street, New York,
New York 10014, USA • Penguin Group (Canada), 90 Eglinton Avenue East, Suite 700,
Toronto, Ontario M4P 2Y3, Canada (a division of Pearson Penguin Canada Inc.) •
Penguin Books Ltd, 80 Strand, London WC2R 0RL, England • Penguin Ireland,
25 St Stephen's Green, Dublin 2, Ireland (a division of Penguin Books Ltd) •
Penguin Group (Australia), 707 Collins Street, Melbourne, Victoria 3008, Australia
(a division of Pearson Australia Group Pty Ltd) • Penguin Books India Pvt Ltd, 11
Community Centre, Panchsheel Park, New Delhi–110 017, India • Penguin Group (NZ),
67 Apollo Drive, Rosedale, North Shore 0632, New Zealand (a division of Pearson New
Zealand Ltd) • Penguin Books, Rosebank Office Park, 181 Jan Smuts Avenue,
Parktown North 2193, South Africa • Penguin China, B7 Jaiming Center, 27 East Third
Ring Road North, Chaoyang District, Beijing 100020, China

Penguin Books Ltd, Registered Offices: 80 Strand, London WC2R 0RL, England

First trade paperback edition 2012
Copyright © 2011 by Julia Cameron

Most Tarcher/Penguin books are available at special quantity discounts for bulk
purchase for sales promotions, premiums, fund-raising, and educational needs. Special
books or book excerpts also can be created to fit specific needs. For details, write
Penguin Group (USA) Inc. Special Markets, 375 Hudson Street, New York, NY 10014.

The Library of Congress catalogued the hardcover edition as follows:

Cameron, Julia.
The prosperous heart: creating a life of "enough" / Julia Cameron with Emma Lively.
p.   cm.
ISBN 978-1-58542-897-7
1. Creative ability.   2. Finance, personal.   3. Spiritual life.   I. Lively, Emma.   II. Title.
BF408.C1756   2011   2011039727
650.1—dc23

ISBN 978-0-399-16198-8 (paperback edition)

Printed in the United States of America
1   3   5   7   9   10   8   6   4   2

BOOK DESIGN BY AMANDA DEWEY

Some of the names and identifying characteristics of the people featured in this book have
been changed to protect their privacy.

While the author has made every effort to provide accurate telephone numbers and Internet
addresses at the time of publication, neither the publisher nor the author assumes any responsibility for errors, or for changes that occur after publication. Further, the publisher does
not have any control over and does not assume any responsibility for author or third-party
websites or their content.

PROSPERITY PRAYER

Oh, Great Creator,
I prosper through you, drawing my abundance from your infinite stores.
You know my needs and you provide for them.
You know my dreams, and you bring me their fulfillment.
I rely on you as my source.
You are the rock on which I build my life.
I trust you to supply me with all things necessary to my happiness.
You are my security. I turn to you always.
Guard and guide me.
Amen.

CONTENTS

THIS BOOK IS DEDICATED TO GERARD HACKETT,
WHOSE FRIENDSHIP IS BOTH OLD AND GOLD.

—Julia Cameron

INTRODUCTION

It was an early fall day, crisp and sunny. I had just moved into my eleventh-floor apartment on the Upper West Side of Manhattan. I woke up with the feeling of being watched. Sure enough, a huge bird was perched on my fire-escape railing, staring in at me. I stared back. Could it be an eagle? In New York City? Amazingly, it was. In Native American lore, the eagle is a symbol of power. I took this eagle to be the symbol for New York: powerful, aggressive, assertive, pressing in on me. The bird raised its wings, posing—like the seal of the president of the United States, the image on the quarter, the image on the dollar bill—as if to trumpet, "I am prosperity."

People think of prosperity as a fiscal bottom line. "When I have X amount of money, I will feel better." The truth is that prosperity is a spiritual bottom line, and the formula should actually be, "When I have X amount of *faith*, I will feel better."

Prosperity at its root is a belief in a benevolent something—and a belief that that "something" will guide us and guard us. We will be led in the direction of good no matter what amount of money we have at our disposal. Prosperity is *never* just about money.

In my personal history, I have had tight fiscal times and times of greater abundance. I have learned to have a sense of safety based on my conviction that God will provide. But this is not a pie-in-the-sky fantasy. Looking back, *always,* when a demand for cash has appeared, the supply of cash has appeared also. What may appear beyond my means is not beyond the means of the Higher Power. This does not mean that when I wish for something expensive, God provides it like Santa Claus. It simply means that a prosperous heart—and everything we need—is always available to us. Sometimes, when we think we need a bigger paycheck, what we really need is change. In knowing our spending patterns, we know ourselves. Prosperity is not just about money—but to have a prosperous heart, our relationship to money must be brought out into the light, and we must be brave enough to look candidly at it.

In this book, I will use the word *God*. You may substitute *Good Orderly Direction, flow,* even *prosperity*. Do not let semantics be a block for you. You don't need to believe in an anthropomorphic God to experience a prosperous heart or use the tools in this book. If you can't believe in the boldness of an eagle, try believing in a hummingbird instead. That smidgen of faith is enough.

Why a prosperity book? I have taught creative unblocking for thirty-five years. When I ask my students about money, inevitably the response is emotional. "Money is the biggest block to my creativity," "I feel like I can handle anything but money," and, "Do we *have* to talk about money?" are common exclamations.

Yes. We have to talk about money.

I believe that every person is creative, and can use his or her creativity to create a life of "enough." I myself have worried about money—and found that having money does not end this worry. I have also discovered practical tools that have brought my students—and myself—out of money worry, out of an anxious heart and into a prosperous one. I believe that prospering is something we can *do*, right now, today, no matter how much money we have.

When we look closely, have we ever *really* been left high and dry? A colleague of mine lost her entire fortune to a Ponzi scheme run by a nefarious financier. On the day he went to jail in handcuffs, she didn't know whether she could keep her house. Her available liquid assets were so low that she was terrified to spend a dime. And what happened? Friends, family, colleagues, strangers reached toward her, offering to bring her and her husband into their homes, offering to give them money, offering to cook, to lend, to listen. The generos-

"There is only one way by which you can achieve prosperity. It is to take charge of your mind."
—ERIC BUTTERWORTH

ity of the people around her stunned her. But I was not surprised. She is a leader who has always been generous with her knowledge, her vulnerability, her wisdom. Her good—her *prosperity*—was coming back to her tenfold. To my eye, God was speaking through these people to her.

"But, Julia!" my students protest when I ask them to consider that they are not alone with their financial problems or secrets, no matter how dire they may feel. "How can you have faith that some abstract something is looking out for our *money*?"

From the front of the room, I can see that my students are visibly uncomfortable in this territory. It sounds too simple, too naïve, too . . . crazy. Ask God to help with their finances? Have I lost my mind? But I stand firm, letting the room explore the beliefs that we as a culture accept without question.

"I'd have more faith if I had more money. If the deal I have pending comes through, I'll believe that something is looking out for me," one student stubbornly asserts.

"Isn't it easier to have faith when you have money?" another one chimes in.

Although we sometimes *imagine* it would be easier to have faith if we had more money, this is a misplaced faith, a belief in dollars and cents instead of a belief in a caring universe. Faith must be placed squarely in the lap of the Higher Power. How do we do that? The swiftest way is through affirmative prayer—prayer in which we affirm that we are led and provided for. There is always enough. But we have a responsibility, too: we can pray to catch the bus, but we still have to run like hell! We have to take action. We have to bring our numbers out into the light, shake hands with them, invite them to tea, ask them how they are today. And ask our money how it is serving us, how we are serving ourselves.

"We could rightly say that how we think and feel about our 'troubles' is critical to our keeping ourselves in a prosperity consciousness."
—ESTHER AND JERRY HICKS

What we are after is clarity, serenity, a sense of safety—this is a prosperous heart.

Last Saturday I had a date with a writer friend of mine. As we strolled through the Santa Fe Farmers Market, past bins of succulent produce, she told me that she had recently finished a new book proposal and that four companies were vying for it. This would seem like good news, but no—my friend was worried. "Nobody has any money these days. I wonder how much I'll get."

My friend owns her own house and has a lucrative coaching practice. She is far better off than many people, but a lack of money haunts her. She is full of blunt questions: "How much money did you get for your new book? How much money do you make teaching?"

My answer to both questions is, "Enough," but that does little to steer the conversation to sunnier climes. No, my friend predicts impending doom for both of us, and any telltale optimism on my part is put down to denial. To hear my friend tell it, realism and pessimism are one and the same. She is habituated to worry, and worry about money is the most deeply grooved worry of all.

Although our culture invites us to dwell on negativity, there is an alternative that we can encourage in ourselves. That alternative is the prosperous heart. The prosperous heart recognizes that prosperity is a spiritual bottom line, not a fiscal one. Our faith, not our cash flow, is what brings to our lives comfort and ease.

Over the next twelve weeks, you will meet yourself and your finances. You will cover spiritual and financial terrain that may sometimes be bumpy, but ultimately will take you on a path to viewing yourself, your dreams, and your finances with more clarity and more faith.

HOW TO USE THIS BOOK

In 1992 I published a book called *The Artist's Way: A Course in Discovering and Recovering Your Creative Self*. Nineteen years later, I still teach this course regularly, online and in person. The need seems to be as great now as it ever was, and inevitably, one topic in particular seems to be loaded for my students. That topic is money.

Over lunch with my publisher, Joel Fotinos, I broached the idea for a new course, a course that is about money, but that is about something more than money: true prosperity.

"What is true prosperity, in your view?" Joel asked. Joel has always been a muse for me, and his thoughtful questions and keen ear inspired the shape of this book.

"I think prosperity is about having 'enough'—having a life beyond need and worry," I told him. "It's about more than prosperity in financial terms. It's more about being satisfied, about having a prosperous *heart*."

And so, a course that is about money—and not about money. A course that is about more than money—about having a prosperous heart—about finding satisfaction in our lives, improving the lives we have, and creating a life of "enough."

And yes, straightening out your finances, too.

This book is a twelve-week course, divided into twelve chapters. I suggest that you work through a chapter a week. Be gentle with yourself: a chapter a week is fast enough. Some of the essays within the chapters will include short exercises for you to complete as you go through the book. At the end of each week, there is a check-in and a list of "prosperity points": do as many as you can. You do not have to do all of them—and in deciding which exercises to do, choose the ones you are most attracted to and the ones you are most resistant to. Our resistance often points us toward "pay dirt." Commit yourself to trying the tools for twelve weeks. The results may surprise you: I often find that when my students shake the apple tree, oranges fall. And oranges may have been just what they were looking for after all.

THE BASIC TOOLS

Prosperity is a spiritual matter. It is the amount of faith we have, not cash, that determines our feelings of abundance. Following are a few simple tools that will cultivate feelings of prosperity in us. You will recognize two of them (Morning Pages and Walking) as classic Artist's Way tools you have used before in other incarnations. They have been refashioned for this program with a stronger emphasis on developing a prosperous heart. Through the use of all of these tools, we become solvent. The key to prosperity is spiritual willingness. It takes willingness to commit to using the tools. You may feel intense resistance to some of them. Simply acknowledge your feelings of resistance; then move ahead anyhow. The degree of resistance you feel is often in direct proportion to the usefulness and value of the tool you resist.

MORNING PAGES

Morning Pages are the primary tool of a creative recovery. They are also a primary tool for establishing prosperity. Three daily pages of longhand writing, strictly stream of consciousness, they provoke, clarify, comfort, cajole, prioritize, and synchronize the day at hand. This daily writing, coupled with Counting, will bring you to emotional—and financial—clarity. You will discover your true values—personal and monetary—and uncover the actions that will lead you to a life that is truly your own.

Morning Pages are to be written by hand—no speeding ahead by computer. They are to be done first thing in the morning, and they are to be shown to no one. They are private; they are personal; they are important. Best done on 8.5 x 11–inch lined paper, they are three single-sided pages. Do not be tempted to use a smaller journal—smaller pages tend to also make your thoughts smaller. Conversely, be sure to stop at three pages. As tempting as it may be to keep writing, it is important not to overdo. We do not want to become so immersed in exploring our psyches that we fail to act in our lives. Three pages are enough to make deep changes, while also maintaining a functional existence in the world. Write about absolutely anything, and if it is hard to think of what to write, write, "I can't think of what to write." Just keep writing. There is no wrong way to do Morning Pages.

"Today I recognize the abundance of life. I animate everything in my experience with this idea."
—Ernest Holmes

A day at a time, a page at a time, we explore our lives, seeking to make our expenditures of time and money align with our personal value system. Morning Pages are like getting up in the morning and telephoning yourself. Not only are you contacting yourself, you are also contacting your *self*. Over time, Morning Pages lead to a sense of wisdom and a nurturing belief in the benevolence of universal flow. Just what do we mean by that? Morning Pages allow us to move through our lives with greater ease. There is an intermeshing of our inner and outer worlds.

At first, Morning Pages may seem negative. "All I do is gripe!" you might exclaim. Reluctant to create—or perpetuate—negativity, you may wish to avoid "meeting your shadow." But suppressing negativity only allows it to fester; by contrast, dumping your negativity onto the page each morning lets your shadow get in its two cents' worth rather than allowing it to darken your whole day.

Morning Pages are very powerful: you may experience them as a propulsive flow, a sort of creative river underlying all of life. They will become a best friend, a safe place to vent, to celebrate, to mourn, to wish. Although at first doing it may take some getting used to—getting up half an hour earlier, carving out an uninterrupted window before the day begins—Morning Pages quickly become a sort of positive addiction. I have been doing Morning Pages now for thirty years. On the rare occasion that I miss a day, I find myself out of sorts and slightly removed from the day at hand. My students have experienced the same thing: the act of doing Morning Pages "clears the slate" on a daily basis—leaving us available to be present in our day and, ultimately, in our lives.

Morning Pages are intended to both challenge and comfort us. In our pages, we ask questions and receive answers. The "still, small voice" grows louder and clearer as we go inside to hear it. Clarity is the reward of Morning Pages. We know what we want and why. Over time, we are guided to action. The actions we choose to take, however small, will ultimately lead us to create a deeply, thoughtfully handmade life.

COUNTING

The bedrock tool of prosperity is a very simple one: Counting. You are asked to keep a ledger—a small notebook will do—of money in and money out. Counting brings clarity, and clarity is one of the first and finest fruits of prosperity. No amount of money is too small or too large to be counted. The loan you make to your brother and the packet of gum you buy at the newsstand are both subject to recording. The unexpected bonus from work, the inheritance check from your late aunt's estate—these, too, must be counted. Counting is an old-fashioned tool. Many of our elders practiced it. You will be joining a time-honored tradition, so let yourself count.

"We have been taught to believe that negative equals realistic, and positive equals unrealistic."
—Susan Jeffers

ABSTINENCE

The third basic tool might be seen as a nontool: stop debting. We call this tool *Abstinence*. Before practicing Abstinence, our life is like a boat with a leak. When we commit to practicing Abstinence, we plug the leak, and the boat stops sinking. Abstinence means no more borrowing ahead on paychecks—no more borrowing, period. No more loans for which we have no collateral. A house loan or a car loan is permissible—as long as the house or car we choose has a monthly payment that we can afford. But we cannot indulge in loans for our rent or basic services. While this may seem severe, it leads straight to prosperity. It's hard to feel prosperous when we are debting.

WALKING

The fourth tool is a deceptively simple one. Unlike Counting and Morning Pages, it requires no intellectual effort. What is this tool? Walking. Walk at least twice a week, for a minimum of twenty minutes. You will discover when you walk that many events fall into a healthier perspective. You may walk out with a problem and walk back in with a solution.

Walking is an opportunity to immerse yourself in the present. You may set out distracted by your thoughts, but you will soon become interested by the details of your surroundings. Walking is an opportunity to enjoy the beauty of the world—the cat on the windowsill, the window box filled with velvety petunias, the forsythia bush flaring gold in early spring, the mother pushing a stroller, the lovers strolling hand in hand, the elderly couple sitting side by side on a bench, the cocker spaniel puppy plunging ahead on its leash—all these sights and more fire your imagination. You are replenishing your inner well, stocking it with sights and sounds.

"You may trust love to get you out of your difficulties. There is nothing too hard for it to accomplish for you, if you put your confidence in it."

—Charles Fillmore

There is a benevolent Something interconnecting all of life. We sense that Something when we walk. Walking is a time-honored spiritual tradition. Native Americans walk on vision quests, aborigines go on walkabouts, Wiccans trace the ley lines. Walking brings a welcome sense of connection. It brings optimism and increases energy. Walking gives a sense of health and well-being.

Walking here in Santa Fe, I startle a lizard, which scoots off the path. I feel a sense of magic. My heart leaps up. The lizard's unexpected beauty announces Mother Nature—always powerful, always surprising. It is common when we walk to experience a sense of expansion. Walking is a luxury, an escape from our frantic pace. When we walk, we experience the richness of the world. When we walk, we experience our own inner prosperity.

TIME-OUT

The fifth tool is a "Time-Out." Once in the morning and once at night, take five minutes to sit quietly. You may use this time to consciously count your blessings. You may use this time to simply rest. Time-Outs put us in touch with our own inner resources. They help us to know how we are feeling and why. Time-Outs give us the chance to review our choices. In sitting quietly with ourselves for a moment, we are able to reassess our day and begin anew. Ideas often come to us in our Time-Outs that prove to be efficient and guided.

A deliberate Time-Out offers us a chance for self-appraisal and self-approval. We may feel a sense of conscious contact with a benevolent universal source. I am often asked whether prayer and meditation count as Time-Outs. Yes, you may use this time to pray. I am also sometimes asked whether taking a Time-Out will allow self-critical thoughts to emerge. My experience has been that it

"I do everything with a sense of reliance upon the Law of Good; therefore, I know that my word shall not return unto me void."
—ERNEST HOLMES

does not. Time-Outs tend not to put us in touch with a critical, ego-driven voice, but rather to put us in touch with a deeper, kinder, wiser part of ourselves. The point is to stop what you are doing and take a moment to listen to yourself think. I suspect that what you hear will be encouraging.

Week One

THE
MONEY MYTH

This week, you will be looking at your spending habits as you begin incorporating the basic tools into your life. Morning Pages will bring you mental clarity on a daily basis. Counting will provide you with financial clarity, as well. Do not be disturbed by strong emotions you may feel as you begin. You are turning on the windshield wipers and allowing yourself to "see" your life as it exists. Some things you see may disturb you. Other things may anger or confuse you. Keep writing. Keep Counting. A day at a time, do not debt. Clarity and peace will come.

You will also be introduced to the different spending personalities, and identify yourself in one (or sometimes more than one) of the categories. As you bring your money habits gently into the light, other insights are likely to surface, as well. You will begin to explore what your anxiety about money has been masking. Worry about money is one of the primary blocks to creativity, and you are likely to find great relief as you discover that you are closer to having a prosperous heart than you think.

ON COUNTING

"The universe will reward you for taking risks on its behalf."
—Shakti Gawain

Prosperity has nothing to do with money. So let's talk about money.

The bedrock prosperity tool, which you will be using for the duration of this book, is called Counting. In Debtors Anonymous, this tool is called "recording" or "keeping your numbers," and that is exactly what you will do. Begin with the purchase of a small spiral notebook—small enough to fit in your pocket or purse. Date page one and begin by recording the precise cost of the notebook. Throughout the rest of the day, keep precise track of your money in and your money out. This tool brings you objectivity. You are asked to observe and record your spending patterns. You may notice that you tell yourself you haven't got enough money for the most basic supplies, like groceries. And yet, in black and white, you can see your daily Starbucks habit: $3.19 for an iced coffee. Counting tells you whether you are spending along the lines of your true values. Often, we are not.

You may tell yourself you have no money to go to the movies, but there in black and white you see that you have a weekly tabloid habit. You read addictively about the lives of others. You buy four magazines detailing the royal wedding of William and Kate. By the end of the month, you have spent your movie money. You've clogged your mind with gossip, and you've cluttered your home with junk magazines.

Often, our expenditures are a revelation to us, and we may find ourselves looking for a loophole—a way to spend without "really" spending. So yes, the charge we put on our husband's credit card is money spent. Big expenditures—the rent, the car payment, the insurance—are also "money out." All expenditures, large or small, are recorded in black and white.

But what about "money in"? Precisely the same rule applies. We count every penny. We record the dime we found on the sidewalk, and the payment for work performed. No amount is too petty—or too large. We record, too, the money that seems to us to be "free money." This is the inheritance we weren't expecting, the bonus above and beyond our pay. This money, too, is real. We record the sudden influx thankfully.

Counting is a tool that works for *everyone.* My student Jocelyn pleaded with me not to count her money in and money out. A "trust-fund baby," she received $5,000 monthly. It was enough for her to live on—yet it didn't feel as though the money were really hers. She felt shame at her lack of earnings. She brought no money in except her monthly stipend. Jocelyn often worked, but she worked for free, helping others with their projects and drawing no salary for her input and ideas. The first month of Counting, Jocelyn became aware that she needed to bill for her time and expertise. At first she underpriced her talents, yet when she was paid even a fraction of her worth, she was nearly ecstatic. She had "money in" for her labors.

"I didn't want to count," Jocelyn recalls. "I was afraid to record my expenditures. I worried that I was spoiled. I felt guilty that I didn't *need* to work. Counting taught me that I *wanted* to work. I realized I was giving away my time and my talents. Unconsciously, I think because I didn't need to be paid, I felt I didn't deserve to be paid."

In a workshop, I relate my own experience: how I told myself I had no money for theater tickets; then realized that if I spent less money buying plays to read, I would have ample money to buy the tickets I so coveted. I ask for more questions on the tool of Counting. One woman raises her hand.

"When I'm out with my husband, the money we spend comes from his wallet. Does that count?"

"The present moment is filled with joy and happiness. If you are attentive, you will see it."
—THICH NHAT HANH

"Listen to your own Self.
If you listen to that Self
within, then you
find the Truth."

—Kabir

"Yes," I tell her. "He's spending for both of you."

Another woman raises her hand. "I have money deposited automatically into my account. Does that count?"

"Yes," I tell her. "It does count. You need to become more conscious, so those funds should be earmarked 'money in.'"

One more woman raises her hand. "You want me to keep track of the money I loan my brother or the petty cash I give my kids?" she asks. She laughs, adding, "I think I know the answer."

"Yes," I tell her. "All of it counts."

Counting makes us conscious about money. We often find our spending pattern is out of sync with our values. Counting shows us where we are out of alignment. It brings us much-needed clarity. Over time, it brings us hope. If you have resistance to Counting, be gentle with yourself. You are noticing, not judging. Counting is an exercise in self-observation, not self-flagellation.

You need not tally these numbers or do anything other than watch them. The insights you need will reveal themselves to you. Counting always, in time, lessens our anxiety over money.

Resistance to clarity comes from fear. We think that we would "rather not know," but ignorance is not bliss. It is anxiety. As simple as this tool is, it is the bedrock on which we build purposeful and dignified lives. Prosperity begins with clarity.

Take yourself out to buy your Counting notebook. Be sure to record its price. Most people prefer a small, pocket-size spiral-bound notebook. This can fit into your pocket or be carried with your wallet. The point is to find something you will enjoy using. Maggie found a small spiral notebook with a deer on its front cover. "Like Bambi," she said. Michael found a notebook with a jet. "I wanted my finances to soar," he said. Kaitlin chose a notebook with a blank cover—"Green, the color of money." And . . . of hope.

WHAT'S YOUR SPENDING TYPE?

Counting brings clarity. Clarity entails self-knowledge. As you count, you will begin to see your spending patterns. Knowledge of your patterns is the beginning of control. There are four basic spending types. Which are you?

The Big-Ticket Spender

The first type is what I call the "Big-Ticket Spender." Money goes for status symbols. A Burberry raincoat, Prada shoes, Coach handbags—anything with an expensive and recognizable label. Chanel sunglasses, a Missoni sweater, an Armani suit. The Big-Ticket Spender is trying to buy self-worth. "See how important I am?" says the Rolex watch, the Tiffany ring. The Big-Ticket Spender wants to purchase status. Status symbols give this spender a sense of security. "See how well I'm doing?" the labels ask. "Don't question me too closely," his finery declares. "Nothing but the best is good enough for me." In reality, however, just beneath the surface lurk insecurity and anxiety about performance.

Clark was a Big-Ticket Spender. Always dressed to the nines, he tried to exude success. At dinners out, he insisted on picking up the check. His credit cards were often maxed out, and it was always a surprise to him when one was declined. He always had a "big deal" pending—a deal that would put him far into the black. Meanwhile, he operated far in the red. Forever shocked when his finances were questioned, he had a loyal wife who worked to bring in money for both of them. But her earnings were not enough to cover his extravagances. He spent against the "big deal" he was sure was coming. He borrowed funds he could not repay. He lived in borrowed houses, on borrowed time. He sought to involve his more solvent friends in his shaky money dealings.

"The Fillmores taught that prosperity is governed by the same laws that govern physical health. They thought that if they could maintain themselves in a prosperity consciousness, an awareness of God as the Source of their supply, prosperity could not fail to be theirs."
—James Dillet Freeman

Finally, he went one step too far, asking his friends to help him cover up an illegal deal that was starting to unravel. Instead of joining him in his lies, a friend reported him to the police. Now Clark is in jail, which hasn't stopped his scheming. His wife loyally defends him, claiming it was all a misunderstanding and a mistake. "Clark will fix everything once he is free."

The truth, of course, is the opposite. Clark will continue to chase big deals. Even from jail he is plotting and planning the big deal that will solve it all.

"I am worthy of having money."
—PATRICIA BASS

The Bargain Buyer

Our second type of spender is what we call the "Bargain Buyer." Quantity, not quality, gives this type a sense of security. Following fads, this spender buys items that are *like* high-ticket items, and feels a sense of self-worth from owning up-to-the-minute fashions. This is the shopper who frequents Filene's Basement, one eye out, always, for the "deal." Spotting a bargain, this shopper must have it—whether the item is needed or not. This shopper masks anxiety with compulsive bargain hunting. If the sweater's on sale, it's a good buy whether it's flattering or not. Very often, this shopper prides herself on shrewdness. "Wait until you see how well I did."

The Bargain Buyer is a compulsive shopper in disguise. Although the Bargain Buyer does shop compulsively, this type of spender rationalizes her purchases because of the "great deal" she is getting. Different from the Big-Ticket Spender, who buys to impress, the Bargain Buyer believes she deserves only what she can buy at a discount—and then she deserves it in bulk.

Madelyn is a Bargain Buyer. Mired in an unhappy marriage, she uses the temporary high of shopping to mask her predicament. A fight with her husband and she's off to medicate her grief with needless purchases to make her feel like her marriage is solid—which it is not.

"Look what I found," she will crow to friends, showing them a new pair of shoes just like last week's. "And you won't believe what a deal I got!" She often buys duplicates of things that strike her fancy. Her house is crammed to the rafters, and she often complains that she needs a still larger house to hold all her loot. At any suggestion that she overshops, she protests that not only are her new purchases necessary, but she saved lots of money by buying them on sale.

The Monetary Miser

The third spending type is called the "Monetary Miser." This is the shopper who doesn't make purchases, even when they are called for. "I can get by with what I've got" is this shopper's motto, and so shabbiness becomes a badge of honor. "I'm above the shopaholic in my spiritual attainment." What is this shopper masking? Not spiritual attainment, but a lack of faith in the future. Rather than declare, "I am deserving of good, and as I work hard and take care of my finances, I trust that I will be guided to right action and safety," the Monetary Miser trusts no one. Chronically worried about the future, he fails to enjoy the present.

Bernice is a Monetary Miser. She overworks, underspends, and considers herself a virtuous person. She frequents secondhand shops and dresses in her "finds." Miserly with herself as well, she underbills for her services and refuses to spend money on her own behalf. Not for her the manicure and pedicure that bespeak self-worth. Not for her the timely haircut. She seldom dines out and prides herself on her frugal ways. Feeling superior and calling these expenditures showy and wasteful, she masks her insecurity with her pride. She is stubbornly independent, turning away the small joys that would be

"This is a rich universe and there is plenty for all of us."
—UNKNOWN

the very things to bring her more optimism. Judging others, she wears a martyr's cloak.

The Enabler

There is a fourth spending pattern that is well worth noting. It entails trying to medicate the anxiety of another through spending our own money on their behalf. Enablers often take responsibility for debts and expenditures that are not their own. To the Enabler, money is love. The idea of saying no is frightening. The Enabler is afraid that the other person will read their *no* as "I don't love you." The Enabler's spending pattern is actually masking a lack of confidence in the strength of his relationships. Enablers do not want to appear selfish, and so will consistently place others' needs first, fearing that if they assert themselves, they will lose their friends and lovers. No matter how much money Enablers earn, none of it brings a sense of security, since they may be tapped for a loan at any moment. The Enabler often feels victimized. Anger simmers just below the surface. The Enabler wants to say no, but is afraid of the imagined consequences. To Enablers, changing their enabling ways would mean losing everything they have.

When Mark married Susan, he married her spending habits, as well. Susan liked to live beyond her means, and Mark liked to support her spending. At first he took pride in being able to provide her with luxuries. But as time wore on and her spending steadily increased, Mark found himself worrying about basic finances. Susan would buy a Tiffany lamp while Mark struggled to pay the electric bill. Susan coveted a home in a gated community. The home was beyond Mark's means, and he knew it, but he was afraid to draw a line. He still believed that money could buy Susan's love, and Susan encouraged him to believe that. Against his better judgment, Mark purchased Susan's expensive house. When it came time to furnish it, Susan's extravagance seemed to know no bounds. Mark protested the charge-card purchases, and Susan complained that he was being "cheap." She hired a designer and, before long, embarked on a love affair. Mark was suspicious, but he continued to pay the bills. This lasted until he came home early and discovered his wife in their costly designer bed with their costly designer. All Mark's money had not bought him loyalty.

As you recognize your spending type, the specific anxiety it masks becomes clearer. Counting helps you first to recognize, and then to abort self-destructive patterns. You may find yourself spending less, or spending more wisely. Counting adjusts your attitudes toward money, performing a sort of monetary realignment. At different times you may find yourself falling into different patterns, seeking to block your anxiety by adopting whichever type feels most comfortable in the moment.

Compulsive spending is always masking something else—and we spend compulsively *because* we are trying so hard to mask something else. As painful, as dark, as isolating as it can be to be financially out of control, it is a familiar pain, and one that is *temporarily* soothed by the unhealthy spending behavior. But inevitably, the bills come, the pain comes back, and spending again will not cure the root anxiety. If we are over- or underspending to numb our feelings of low self-worth, of false pride, of anxiety about relationships, or to fill a spiritual emptiness within, we are not addressing the root cause of the feelings themselves.

Make no mistake: any and all of these patterns mask an inner anxiety. We must learn to ask ourselves, "What am I afraid of?" When the answer becomes clear, we must learn to take that fear to our spiritual source, asking our Higher Power to intervene.

DEBT

"I refuse to worry about anything. I have complete confidence that the God who is always with me is able and willing to direct everything I do, to control my affairs, to lead me onto the pathway of peace and happiness."

—Ernest Holmes

If our spending habits mask anxiety, they also create anxiety. And the most anxiety-provoking behavior of all is to debt. "I'm living on my credit cards," Mary says, little realizing that the debt she accrues will come to bear. Credit-card debt is an American epidemic. "Charge it," we say when we feel low on cash. We'll pay the bills off when we have more money, we tell ourselves. But when will that be? We use our credit cards to inflate our incomes. We use them to feel solvent when we are not. Many of us play credit-card roulette, loading one card to its maximum and then moving on to the next. "It's the American way," we say, opening our mailbox to find notices that we've qualified for still more cards and more debt.

Meanwhile, we may not even be able to pay our cards' minimum. We may fear the telephone, afraid that our creditors are calling. We find ourselves, yet again, at a checkout counter, eyeing the purchase that we don't need but *feel* we need, wishing we knew what the balance was on the card but actually having no idea. When our card is declined, we are defensive, angry. We tell the clerk she must have typed a number wrong, that our accountant is behind on bill payment, that "something is wrong with the card." What is wrong is that *we* have maxed the card out. Conversely, when the charge is accepted, we feel a surge of excitement, a sense of relief, of entitlement. "See, I deserved to buy that. I can afford it." But spending on credit has nothing to do with being able to afford something. And the anxiety that credit-card debt creates is something we cannot afford. Anxiety over debt cannot coexist with true prosperity.

What can we do about the anxiety that a debt load creates? We can stop debting. Yes—that's right—no debting. At all. Not all of us use credit cards, but there are other ways we debt that are not healthy for us. We can inventory our own type of debting. Do you borrow from friends? Do you borrow ahead on your pay? Do you live on credit cards? Do you write checks against money coming in?

One day at a time, for the duration of this book, do not debt. Do not buy anything for which you could not pay cash on the barrelhead. If you use a credit card for a purchase, deduct that money from your bank account and pay it off immediately. Just for today, focus on the present. Do not beat yourself up about your past debting behavior. Focus on the now. Expect that as you stop debting, you will enter into a withdrawal period. Expect sudden bursts of anger. As your sense of financial self-worth returns, you will expect other people in your life to behave responsibly around money, too. You are changing rapidly. Those around you must change, too. As you stop trying to buy self-worth, you will find yourself feeling it.

Karen earned good money as a buyer, but no matter her salary, she chronically spent more than she earned. Karen was a Big-Ticket Spender, convinced she always had to carry the latest bag, no matter what the cost. She panicked when she stopped debting.

"I thought I'd never be chic again," Karen says with a laugh. Imagine her surprise when she received an unexpected bonus from work. It precisely covered the cost of her newest coveted handbag— and matching shoes. "Maybe there's something to this not debting," she thought, as she rushed out to make her purchases.

"A wise man never loses anything if he has himself."
—Montaigne

Arriving at her favorite store, she scooped up the handbag, only to find herself thinking, "Do I really need this?" Ditto for the shoes. For the first time in her memory, she left the store empty-handed. Feeling giddy, she drove to the bank and opened her first savings account, depositing the check there instead.

"I feel like I have become a believer," Karen gushed. "I'm all right without the latest and the greatest. And I'm more excited about this savings account than I ever felt about a handbag."

"For several centuries now, we have overemphasized the intellect. It is fine in its place. It is not, however, the most authentic way of knowing. The most authentic comes from the heart."

—SONIA CHOQUETTE

Another student, Richard, listened to Karen's story with jealousy, feeling that if he made the kind of money she did, he would easily be able to rectify his finances.

"I'm spending money on food, not handbags," he mumbled resentfully.

With encouragement and great reluctance, Richard tried not debting. He earned an erratic salary as a graphic designer, and made up for "lean times" by living off his credit card. Lately, his work had been sparse, and his growing debt load kept him constantly uneasy.

"Just try it," I told him.

Reluctantly, he did. Through Counting, he learned that his pricey habit of daily dinners out was keeping his credit card balance consistently beyond his reach.

"I couldn't believe it was so simple," he said. "If I ate out only twice a week, I could be out of credit card debt in a year. What I needed were groceries. The price of a salmon fillet at the supermarket was a third of what I had been paying in a restaurant."

In a year, Richard was out of debt—and he also lost twenty-five pounds.

Financial debt creates a spiritual and emotional debt. Trying to fill the hole in our identity, we often debt more and feel worse. When we stop debting, we are able to forge a new relationship with our Higher Power. Where, before, our credit card was king, we now feel a new sense of relief—some even describe it as a "spiritual experience." The realization that we can stop hurting ourselves financially *does* often feel like a revelation. We can do without, we discover. And often we experience small miracles, as the Higher Power enables us to fulfill our wants without debting. This is true prosperity.

PROSPERITY ISN'T ABOUT MONEY

Almost one hundred percent of the time, when I say that prosperity has nothing to do with money, I am met with snickers, crossed arms, darting eyes. "Of course it does," my students are thinking. I go ahead, inviting my students to voice their skepticism. They are more than willing.

Max, a once-successful businessman, has reluctantly started my course. He is tired of the idea that there is a spiritual solution to what he sees as a very concrete problem. Max is a Big-Ticket Spender, and his big-ticket spending has put him in his midfifties with little to show for his many years of hard work. Max is bitter, resentful. Moving to New Mexico, he has been inundated by—and tried, grudgingly—what he calls "New Age techniques for manifestation."

"I said plenty of affirmations," hisses Max, "and God did not give me a Mercedes." The room explodes with laughter. Max is startled, and then, as if hearing himself for the first time, joins in the laughter as well.

As the laughter dies down, I comment, "I don't blame you for being frustrated. But bear with me. These tools are practical, and they will help you. Are you willing to dig a little deeper?"

Max says yes, tentatively. After all, we are calling his whole life into question.

"Have you ever had a Mercedes?" I ask him, suspecting the answer.

"Yes," says Max. "I collected them. At one point, I had four."

"And did you feel prosperous?"

Max pauses, remembering. "I loved my cars. They were beautiful. But I had bought them on credit, and I always felt like they weren't really mine. Just before my wife left me, I had bought yet another car. It was actually a terrible time in my life and my marriage. And

"Within you is a limitless, unborn potential of creativity and substance. . . . [T]he tragedy can become a blessing, the disadvantage can become an advantage, the failure can become an opportunity and the disappointment can become [God's] appointment."
—ERIC BUTTERWORTH

I did think that another Mercedes would fix everything. What I needed was communication with my wife."

"Let's pause just a minute here," I say. "How many people have thought they could buy their way into intimacy?" Hands shoot into the air. Max is not alone in believing that some "thing" is the answer.

"The desire to be self-supporting and financially independent is a divine desire. . . ."
—Catherine Ponder

"I feel stupid and naïve," Max volunteers. I point out that many of his classmates held the same beliefs he did. We have *all* experienced moments of feeling like the perfect gift would change a situation for the better. We hear of celebrities buying houses and cars for their friends and families, and fantasize about what we would do if we could—and for whom. But true intimacy has nothing to do with money. It has everything to do with honesty. We can *always* take a step toward loving intimacy, in any relationship, without spending a dime.

A SLEUTHING EXERCISE

Set a timer for five minutes. You are purposely giving yourself a short amount of time so that you will write quickly, more easily accessing your subconscious. Write for five minutes on when in your life you felt the most prosperous. There may be one moment or many. Write as fast as you can.

"I felt prosperous when . . ."

Now, glance back through what you have written. Did your feelings of prosperity really have anything to do with money? Most of us find that when we are useful, we feel prosperous. It's not our salary; it's our sense of belonging that matters. The prosperous heart *already* has "enough."

MONEY AND CREATIVITY

For twenty-five years, I have taught a course in creative unblocking called "The Artist's Way." Time and again, I have run up against the cultural belief that artists are broke. Fear of financial hardship keeps many people from exploring their creativity, imprisoning them in jobs they don't like, working for paychecks they tell themselves they are lucky to have. And yet, as people do the work of unblocking, they often find themselves more solvent, not less. Doing something that they love *can* be financially rewarding, much to people's surprise. Often, people must overcome "either-or" thinking—"*Either* I can be creative, *or* I can be solvent." It takes coaxing to get them to take a step toward more creative realms. And yet, opening the doors to their creativity often opens the doors to prosperity, as well.

My student Lisa is a case in point. She worked as an editor at a children's press. The press was prestigious, and Lisa told herself she should be grateful for her job. But she felt stifled and trapped. A wonderful artist in her own right, she could use only part of her skills in her job. Often, she was asked to hire other artists to do work she herself could have done. Beginning a creative recovery, I urged Lisa to try making art in her off-hours. She did as I suggested, and produced a series of watercolors that she entered in a local show. To her surprise, her work sold. Encouraged, she moved ahead rapidly. Soon, her job became a means of support for her art instead of the thing that kept her from it. As her self-worth and, as a result, her reputation as an artist grew, she realized she could make a living as an artist— without her day job. All it would take was a leap of faith. Lisa made that leap, and has supported herself as an artist ever since.

"With God all things are possible."
—Matthew 19:26

When I tell this story, my students are both inspired and intimidated.

"You don't *have* to leave your day job," I reassure them. I tell them about Caroline, a colleague of Lisa's, who chose instead to devote her evenings and weekends to making art.

"I really like having a steady paycheck," Caroline states. "I don't sleep a lot right now, but I'm happy. I know I'm not abandoning my art, but I also know I will be able to pay the rent. Maybe as my art picks up, I will be braver, but for right now, I'm brave enough."

Now, let's take a look at our knee-jerk reactions and cultural assumptions about money. Fill in the following sets of ten sentences as fast as you can. Don't censor yourself. You are looking at underlying beliefs that you carry with you. I have given you a few examples for each to help you get the ball rolling.

"Money is . . ."
1. Money is power.
2. Money is luxury.
3. Money is intimidating.
4. Money is necessary.
5. Money is . . .
   Etc.

"Money means . . ."
1. Money means success.
2. Money means security.
3. Money means I have worked hard.
4. Money means I can pay the bills.
5. Money means I have power.
   Etc.

"Money equals . . ."
1. Money equals strength.
2. Money equals importance.
3. Money equals showing off.

"When you really listen to yourself, you can heal yourself."
—CEANNE DEROHAN

4. Money equals popularity.
5. Money equals snobbery.
   Etc.

"My father thought money was . . ."
1. My father thought money was scarce.
2. My father thought money was the result of working hard.
3. My father thought money was to be "saved for a rainy day."
4. My father thought money was powerful.
5. My father thought money was a reflection of his own value.
   Etc.

"My mother thought money would . . ."
1. My mother thought money would stop my brothers from fighting.
2. My mother thought money would make my father happy.
3. My mother thought money would make her friends jealous.
4. My mother thought money would keep her young.
5. My mother thought money would give her a sense of rest.
   Etc.

"When the mind becomes quiet, you feel nourished."
—SWAMI CHIDVILASANANDA

Take a look at your answers. Is this what you "officially" believe, or do your responses surprise you? Do you see evidence of attitudes you may have about money that stem from your early upbringing? We may feel that our attitudes about money seem both toxic and silly. Don't be fooled. Our attitudes about money always stem from something real—it's just that that something may no longer be relevant to our lives. Someone whose parents grew up in the Great Depression may have been brought up with peculiar attitudes about money that, on the surface, may appear "toxic," but may, upon reflection, make perfect sense. Simply understanding where our attitudes come from can help us overcome—or at least make peace with—them. We may also find that our answers contradict one another. This is okay. Having a complicated relationship with money is not a unique position to be in.

"Everything that I do, say or think today shall be done, said or thought from this spiritual viewpoint— that God, Who is life, is in everything."

—ERNEST HOLMES

WEEK ONE CHECK-IN

Morning Pages: Did you do them this week? How many days?

Counting: Did you count this week? What did you learn?

Abstinence: Did you abstain from debting this week? If you did debt, what was it for? How did you feel?

Walking: Did you walk this week? What insights did you have?

Time-Out: Did you take your Time-Outs? What did you learn?

Prosperity Points

1. Take pen in hand and name your spending type. List three behaviors that helped you to identify your own spending habits. Dig a little deeper and name the basic anxiety you suspect this behavior is masking.

2. Writing as rapidly as you can, respond to the following cues:

1. The reason I can't stop debting is _____

2. The reason I can't stop debting is _____

3. The reason I can't stop debting is _____

4. The reason I can't stop debting is _____

5. The reason I can't stop debting is _____

Survey your list. What behaviors can you change? Which of your answers are irrational? What actions can you take to not debt?

3. Setting aside your skepticism for a moment, make a list of ten actions you could take, right now, that you suspect *might* make you feel prosperous—and that cost nothing.
Example:
   1. Taking a walk in nature
   2. Going for a run and taking a long, hot shower afterward
   3. Cooking soup using leftovers that I have in the house
   4. Cleaning—*really* cleaning—the bathroom, and lighting the candle that I've always "saved" for special occasions
   5. Calling my friend Laura in Chicago
      Etc.

   There are many actions we can take every day that will give us a sense of true prosperity. Choose one action from your list and notice how you feel after you have done it.

4. After finishing these lists, take a solo twenty-minute walk and allow yourself to think about what you just learned regarding your attitudes about money.

HAVING ENOUGH

This week you will be looking back over your habits and beliefs about money. In acknowledging your fears and mourning your losses, you will make way for your true values to emerge. You will address the myths associated with money—that a "magic number" will solve everything, that there's "never enough." In bringing negative emotions into the light and counting the blessings you have received in the past, you will see that there is, already and always, "enough."

ANXIETY

The opposite of prosperity is not poverty. It is anxiety. When we are possessed of a prosperous heart, we do not act rashly out of anxiety. Taking our time, we respond to life rather than merely react to it. Doing so, we find our lives are filled with choices. With these choices comes opportunity. Taking the time to discover it, we find that even apparent adversity has a silver lining.

"But, Julia!" my students protest. "When I am caught in anxiety I can't get out. I can't find the silver lining."

I know. The anxious heart is worried, and the anxious heart is stingy. The revered Buddhist teacher Thich Nhat Hanh advises his students to make a practice of "going home to the home in themselves." He believes that every being has within him a tranquil oasis, free from anxiety. Anxiety and tranquillity cannot coexist. As we practice our basic tools—Morning Pages, Time-Outs, Walks—we become more tranquil; our anxiety abates. In our inner calm, we find that we are *always* safe and secure. Feeling those things, we can turn our attention to the benevolent Something—a sense of deep safety that hovers just at the edge of our consciousness. We find our silver lining by asking to realize the potential good hidden behind the bad. The good is always there to be discovered. Our prayers are always answered, although not necessarily as we had hoped.

Claire is a freelance artist. She lives off her commissions, and has for many years. But Claire is a worrier. Last year, she became so worried that she began having panic attacks and sleepless nights. Fortunately, she had a friend with a prosperous heart. "Why worry?" the friend asked. "Every single time you catch yourself going into worry, go to God instead."

Desperate for relief, Claire tried her friend's advice. "At first it felt really irresponsible," she recalls. "I mean, it just seemed so wrong somehow to just not worry."

Wrong or not, Claire tried to catch herself every time she worried. At first, it was a moment-by-moment practice. She found that she worried nearly all the time. "God's got it," she would tell herself, feeling the habit of worry stubbornly plucking at her psyche. Gradually—very gradually—"God's got it" began to be a fact for her.

"Now I barely worry at all," Claire says. "I catch myself when I do. Worry was a habit for me. Now faith is."

The prosperous heart seeks God. Rather than relying upon itself, the prosperous heart relies upon a Higher Power. Knowing that God is all-powerful, it trusts that some of that power can be channeled in its direction. The prosperous heart knows that God's will and its own are not at opposite ends of the table. Praying for knowledge of

"One day, it was suddenly revealed to me that everything is pure spirit."
—Ramakrishna

"The key to getting the good results that you desire is to manage to feel good even when dollars are in short supply. When you learn to manage the way you feel . . . you will see the law of attraction delivers veritable fortunes to your door. . . . If you will let the improvement in the way you feel be your objective, the greater amounts of money must begin to flow to you. . . ."
—ERIC BUTTERWORTH

God's will and the power to carry it out, the prosperous heart often receives urges to follow a particular direction. In some cases, our heart's desire may be precisely what God has in mind. Other times, God's idea may come as a welcome surprise, steering us onto a new and better course. Either way, a reliance upon God brings welcome results.

No longer at war with ourselves, projecting negatively into the future instead of staying with ourselves in today, we are peaceful. No longer trying to "win," we find ourselves winners. No longer trying to wrest "more" from the world, we find that we have enough. Those whom we meet quickly sense we are not out to vanquish them. They often respond to us with a goodwill that matches our own. We come to expect magnanimity. We wish others well and expect they will wish us well also.

When we stop feeling threatened and reacting out of fear, life ceases to be a roller coaster. Our emotional hills and valleys level out. Operating out of goodwill, we meet our fellows openly and un-guardedly, wishing them the best. This attitude is quickly sensed, and we often find ourselves met in kind. Far from hostile, the world be-gins to feel benevolent. We find ourselves a worker among workers, a friend amid friends. "You're so serene," we may be told. "Serene?" we think doubtfully to ourselves. But we *are* more serene. Others sense this and find it attractive.

When we find ourselves slipping back into anxiety, we need to remind ourselves of our tranquil inner home. We need to extend to ourselves compassion, the same generosity we would extend to an ailing friend.

ADDICTION

Juliette wants to be more creative. She wants to reach inside herself and pull out wonderful ideas. She yearns to work freely, but there's just one bar: Juliette suffers the disease of addiction. Reaching for an idea, she finds herself reaching for "just one" glass of wine.

"A drink will get me past my inner censor," she tells herself. But the first drink takes a second drink, and Juliette's brilliant ideas go glimmering.

Andrew, like Juliette, suffers from addiction. He admits, "I'm a real pothead," and he tells himself that a joint will fire his imagination. But does it? Smoking marijuana, like drinking too much wine, leaves his thoughts muddied. His great ideas become blurred. The clarity necessary for creation eludes him. Frustrated, he smokes another joint, telling himself it is medicinal.

"At least I'm not an alcoholic or a drug addict," Brenda states defiantly. A pretty but pudgy woman, she carries an extra thirty pounds of weight. When a bright idea strikes her and the fierce flow of creative energy courses through her body, she reaches for Häagen-Dazs, telling herself she's hungry when she's not.

Addiction is the disease of masks, the disease of denial. Jim is addicted to novel sexual conquests. He chases a titillating high. Frankie is addicted to work—that is, to *over*work. Mick is a chronic gambler. No matter what form addiction takes, it takes us out of ourselves, and the addiction to money is no different.

"Desire is God tapping at the door of your mind, trying to give you greater good."
—Catherine Ponder

When we addictively spend or hoard money, when we debt or make unsecured loans, we mortgage our lives to anxiety. A deep, sometimes hidden addiction is at play. We call it "being terminally vague." As with the alcoholic or drug addict, a fog settles in. Without Counting, we can't remember where our money went, or why. Our credit card is rejected and we react with shock. We couldn't have charged *that* much, could we? But we have. Each of our other addictions can trigger thoughtless spending, as well.

A sex and love addict, Jim convinced himself that if only Carol were his, all would be right. But how to capture her attention? A new motorcycle—that was the ticket. And so Jim became a Harley-Davidson rider, and his rides took him past the retail store where Carol was manager. As luck would have it, Jim drove by just as Carol was going on break. He waved a friendly hello and piloted his bike to her side.

"Want a ride?" he asked. "Where are you going for lunch? I could take you there." Carol named a local eatery. "Hop on," said Jim, and he drove her to her luncheon spot, where he offered to buy her lunch. Now he had the price of the motorcycle plus the price of Carol's lunch. Driving her back to the store, he asked whether she was free for dinner. To his delight, she agreed to go.

And so a pattern was set. Jim was the big spender, and Carol was the reason why. Carol was "his," until another, wealthier suitor made the scene.

"I can't believe the money I spent," Jim now says ruefully. Entering financial recovery, he is surprised to come face-to-face with his other demons as well.

"I knew I had a problem with debt," Jim muses. "I could never keep up with my credit-card bills. But in Counting, I saw that I frequently tried to buy love. My relationships haven't been healthy. It's going to take me a year just to pay back what I spent on Carol."

Jim is not alone in finding that recovering from a money addiction can reveal other addictions, as well. It takes humility to look closely at our habits. But the prosperous heart is a humble one. It is often during the early weeks of Counting that we first feel the brush of magic. We are, in reality, acutely aware of our finances for perhaps the first time. When we are not debting, the fog lifts and we see clearly for the first time. Not debting, we discover a sense of integrity. We are honorable people, and we acknowledge our daily success.

The prosperous heart is an honest heart. Our humility and our integrity become our strength. Starting with our money, these attributes spread into all areas of our life. As they do, our addictive behaviors no longer serve us.

Now is the time for us to look—gently—at our own addictive patterns. Number from one to five. Fill in the blank:

1. I think I have a problem with _____

2. I think I have a problem with _____

3. I think I have a problem with _____

4. I think I have a problem with _____

5. I think I have a problem with _____

Now, try it again:

1. I know I have a problem with _____

2. I know I have a problem with _____

3. I know I have a problem with _____

4. I know I have a problem with _____

5. I know I have a problem with _____

"They are like trees planted by streams of water, which yield their fruit in its season, and their leaves do not wither. In all that they do, they prosper."

—PSALM 1:3

Admitting our problems is often the first step toward recovery. When we do discover areas where we suspect we may have an addictive pattern or behavior, joining a support group may enable us both to admit defeat and to take positive steps where necessary.

VALUES

"I would say to everyone who wishes to demonstrate prosperity: take God into partnership with you and you will demonstrate abundance."

—CHARLES FILLMORE

I started writing this book on a spring afternoon in New York. The winter was finally over. The cherry trees surrounding the reservoir in Central Park were in full, festive froth. I was perched in my writing chair doing an Artist's Way exercise. I had numbered from one to twenty-five and I was listing—as rapidly as I could—things I love. My list started like this:

1. Sagebrush
2. Piñon
3. Mountains
4. Magpies
5. Eagles
6. Ravens
7. Hawks
8. Vast vistas . . .

I broke off before I was halfway through. Clearly, what I loved was the West, but I was living in Manhattan, which pretty much personifies the East. The irony was not lost on me. I had been living in Manhattan a full decade, a decade full of accomplishment. I had written a book a year, three musicals, and an opera. I had sat in my writing chair, or at the piano, and put pen to page. I had written nearly daily and been well paid for my efforts. I had poured my paychecks into my living expenses—Manhattan is costly—and come out ever so slightly ahead. "What a great apartment," people would say as they set foot in my spacious, sunny domain. There was a wing for me; a wing for Emma, my collaborator; a third wing for work and for guests. "This place is huge," visitors would breathe, measuring the place against their own crowded studios. The place was not "huge," but it was big enough to feel ample, and ample is very nice.

I turned back to my list, determined to include New York.

9.   Korean grocers
10.   Window boxes
11.   The Arthur Ross Pinetum, a pine grove in Central Park
12.   Forsythia bushes
13.   Squirrels

I broke off again. My "New York" list was all flora and fauna. Where was the Chrysler Building, where the Empire State? Surely Madison Avenue deserved a spot? I loved window-shopping its pricey shops.

I started again:

14.   Cowboy boots
15.   Saddles
16.   The Roy-El Morgan Farm—horses!

I was stubbornly back in the West. My New York list was spotty. I tried again:

17.   Bella Luna, an Italian eatery
18.   Pascalou, a French eatery
19.   Sarabeth's, where my friend Judy likes to dine
20.   Big Nick's pizza, home to "New York" pizza

"It is good to have an end to journey towards; but it is the journey that matters, in the end."
—Ursula K. Leguin

I was doing better, but my loves were all sources of comfort foods. What was I comforting myself about? Why did I feel a need to numb my feelings? I was stumbling now on an inconvenient truth:

I was not happy in New York. "Of course you're happy!" I reprimanded myself. "Look how well you're doing!"

But doing well and being well are not the same thing. Despite all my protests, the jig was up. New York no longer matched my needs. I was craving nature, and Central Park would no longer suffice. I craved wildlife, long walks on mountain trails.

I tried to tell Emma, my colleague, how I felt. She didn't understand. She loved New York. The hustle and bustle were tonic to her. The city's manic energy matched her own high-powered pace. She went to the theater. I stayed home. She went to concerts, the opera. I stayed home. Holed up in my room, curled up in my writing chair, I dreamed of a different life:

"There is little sense in attempting to change external conditions, you must first change inner beliefs, then outer conditions will change accordingly."

—BRIAN ADAMS

21. Green chili
22. Tamales
23. The Rio Grande
24. Cliffs
25. A star-spangled sky

Emma tried to interest me in her urban adventures. She'd seen a great new show. She reeled off the credits. I caught myself tuning out. She loved the score. The staging was superb. I was polite but noncommittal. Emma loved Broadway; I dreamed of New Mexico's "Turquoise Trail." Is it any wonder that Emma found herself a new collaborator, someone whose passions matched her own? I felt left out, abandoned . . . and free. My yearnings became clearer. My life in New York merely looked good. It didn't satisfy my heart. My heart felt pinched as I longed for something that felt more generous, more spacious, less rushed. I longed for a prosperous heart.

It is a spiritual axiom that God never closes one door without opening another. The door to Santa Fe swung open as the door to

New York swung closed. Stymied in Manhattan, I turned to the West, where the vistas creatively as well as physically seemed wide-open. My ego longed to stay in New York for the "hipness" factor. My heart yearned for Santa Fe. I chose Santa Fe.

Within three months of making that list, I had moved to Santa Fe. Although that sounds dramatic, and it is, I was fulfilling my heart's desire, and in doing that, I found myself able to be loving and generous. I found myself encouraging others to explore their options for change when they questioned where they were in their lives, able to listen quietly to the musings of my friends and students as they, too, reassessed parts of their lives. Full with my own clarity, my heart was open. Supporting myself by accepting my own true values, I was poised—and now available—to support other people.

"You must have been thinking about Santa Fe a long time," a well-meaning friend remarked to me.

"No," I answered. The idea that seemed so right had come to me suddenly, from out of the blue. The more I held the idea to the light, the more I believed it was the answer. It was an excellent remedy for what ailed me. But the idea was not my own. I'd call it God's.

It was God's idea to delight my heart with beauty. God well knew the price, spiritually, emotionally, and financially, that I had paid for living in New York. I didn't feel that I had *wasted* time or money, but I suspected I would begin to feel that way if I didn't change course. I didn't want to have regrets.

The prosperous heart does not waste time or money. The prosperous heart spends time and money along the lines of its true values.

ON LOSS

Loss is *always* gain in disguise.

If we take this rule to heart, we will find ourselves heading in

> "I am aware of my union with Good. I am conscious of my oneness with Life. I expect more prosperity, more happiness, more harmony than ever before. I walk in the joy of ever-increasing good."
> —ERNEST HOLMES

the right direction. Some loss feels so painful that it cannot easily be seen as gain. This is where faith enters the picture. Taking the time to search for a silver lining, we may find that there is indeed a hidden blessing in our circumstance. "God never gives us more than we can handle," we are told. "Everything happens for a reason." In the moment, it often *does* feel like too much to handle. In the moment, the "reason" may be nowhere to be found. But with a little patience and a glance back through our own stories, we may find that we can trust the beginnings of the faith we are now developing. Seeing loss as gain doesn't mean there isn't a loss to be grieved. But stubbornly choosing to look for the hope or the lesson in even the darkest situation will always lead to growth.

Anita found herself suddenly and savagely in the midst of a divorce. Her husband was sleeping with another woman. He wanted out. At first, Anita was devastated. How could he have betrayed her so? But Anita was resilient. Long dependent on her husband's income, she now looked for—and found—a job of her own. At first, she came home from work exhausted, tumbling into bed at seven p.m., seeking to lose herself in sleep. Within weeks, however, she began to take pride in her performance at work. She began to feel a new self-respect. One long weekend, she took herself to the yarn shop. Before her marriage, back in her single days, she had enjoyed needlepoint. Now she stocked up on needlepoint supplies, and on Monday, after a full day's work, she found herself beginning a project rather than falling into bed.

Tuesday, she caught herself thinking, "I used to be so much faster at this." Wednesday, she felt her skills slowly returning. When a well-meaning neighbor called her to give her an update on her ex-husband's activities, Anita found herself getting quickly off the phone. She didn't want to play victim. She continued to be proud of herself at work, and proud, too, that she had taken up a hobby—her project was a large square pillow featuring a thistle and a butterfly in flight. The thistle symbolized to her the hardship of her situation. The butterfly symbolized her triumph against the odds.

"I had been too dependent on my husband for my identity. My divorce threw me back on my own resources."

Although loss is always painful, it serves to put us in touch with our own spirit. Loss cracks our hard outer shell and exposes our vulnerability. And, exposed, we find that our vulnerability is a source of strength. In touch with our truth, unguarded, we are powerful. Like Anita, we find a vivid inner spirit, a deep core of resilience.

All of us face loss, and loss often comes as a surprise. Our first response is fear, frustration that we didn't see it coming—but we were never expected to see it coming. James was shocked and dismayed when his doctor gave him the unexpected diagnosis of prostate cancer. Always a spiritual man, he found his faith was challenged. "Pray for me," he asked his friends. "Pray for me," he asked his girlfriend of seven years. His operation went smoothly and his surgeon declared it a success. James found himself grateful for the many small blessings in his life, and particularly grateful for the tender care his girlfriend offered him during his recovery.

"She's not a girlfriend; she's a wife," he found himself thinking. He proposed to her and she accepted. Loss of his health actually made him spiritually more whole. James now laughs with wonder and feels his apparent catastrophe brought him wonderful gifts.

"Everything, the smallest good, seems miraculous to me. I can't say I am grateful for my cancer, but I can now see the blessings that it brought into my life, too."

When shifts occur in our financial relationships, the deeper elements of the relationship are often revealed more clearly.

Nathan prided himself on his ability to earn money. He prided himself on spoiling his wife. A fancy home, a fancy car, designer clothes, and a distinguished art collection gave Nathan his sense of identity. Imagine his horror when his investments suddenly went

"Prosperity is not just having things. It is the consciousness that attracts the things."
—ERIC BUTTERWORTH

belly-up. He was the victim of a high-rolling investor. Overnight, his fortunes reversed. With great trepidation, he told his wife, "We're wiped out."

He felt fear. Who was he without his fortune? Would his wife leave him? Willing, despite himself, to be vulnerable, Nathan opened up completely to his wife. He told her of their loss, his fear and shame, his disappointment at not being able to continue to lavish her with beautiful possessions. To his surprise, his wife proved loyal. Her attachment to him was much stronger than her attachment to his gifts. There was indeed much more to their relationship than the trappings of the high life they'd been living.

Relieved and inspired, Nathan found himself possessed of a new-found courage and ingenuity. Rather than bask in bitterness about his investor's betrayal, Nathan rallied his meager resources and—consulting his wife for the first time—made cautious investments in government bonds at the suggestion of a conservative investor—a man without the flash of his previous adviser.

"I don't know that we can rebuild your fortune," Nathan was told. "But we can husband what remains." Talking with his wife, Nathan learned that she had always been fearful they were living in a house of cards. Loss brought Nathan and his wife together. He found their love more valuable than the fortune he had lost.

When Charlotte was told she had been accepted to Juilliard, only to receive a rejection letter in the mail three months later, she called the school, determined to claim her place. When she was told it was too late, she applied to another conservatory at the last minute—one that ended up fitting her needs far more authentically. "I was crushed when I received that letter. It felt so unfair, especially when I was told that it had nothing to do with my audition—I was one of the only people unanimously accepted by the committee—but it was a bureaucratic mistake that couldn't be corrected. But when I went to the other school, the one that seemed so random

"All things I seek are now seeking me."
—Patricia Bass

in the moment, I couldn't believe what a fit it was. I was grateful every day of my master's degree that I wasn't doing it at Juilliard. I am a much smarter and more open-minded musician today because of the environment I ended up in."

Like Charlotte, Anita, James, and Nathan, we may find that hardship forges our character. But we need not lose something valuable to learn the lesson that loss might bring. We need simply to count our blessings, remembering to place human relations ahead of financial gain. We may find ourselves both sane and solvent.

THE MAGIC NUMBER

A number isn't magic. A number is just a number. However, we believe—with all of our being—that a magic number exists, and that getting to it will solve all of our problems. But every time we reach that number, the number is suddenly too low. Why? Because a number will *never* solve all of our problems.

The magic number shimmers on the horizon. We see it as the oasis where all of our problems are solved. The persistence of this illusion is astonishing. Even those of us who feel we are financially sound may still harbor a "magic number" and the belief that it will turn things around.

Marlena had a magic number. It was six figures, and just out of reach, even with raises, for the job she was employed to do. Her number danced enticingly on the horizon, and it kept her from appreciating the very good salary she enjoyed.

Ron, like Marlena, had a magic number. Working on commission as an automobile salesman, he felt the number was within his grasp. Working—and overworking—he reached his magic number, only to discover that his expenses had escalated and his number was now too small.

"The law of receiving is this: Give, then make way to receive."
—Catherine Ponder

Many people experience the phenomenon of a shrinking magic number and an escalating bottom line. Sharon was certain that her magic number would fix her life. Bitterly divorced, she wanted to reach her magic number "to show him." A screenwriter, she believed she would earn respect as well as dollars if she could sell a movie. She was convinced that a movie sale would bring her both public attention as well as financial security, and that she would "win" in the aftermath of the divorce. She fantasized about her magic number—the amount she wished to sell her screenplay for—which she believed would end all of her hardship.

And then the impossible happened: she did sell her screenplay—for slightly more than she had fantasized. At last, she had her magic number. But did she? Somehow, the number was now too small. Bouts of self-attack plagued her, as she wondered whether she had another screenplay in her, wondered whether she had gotten enough for the first one, wondered whether the movie would ever be made. She had missed the joy of the process in the obsession with her payout.

And another thing: she missed the "chase." Now, with her project sold, she lacked focus. When the magic number was still out of reach, she felt fueled by its mirage. Even with the dreamed-of amount of money in her bank account, she hadn't "won." The divorce was still happening; she still had doubt; she still worried about money.

Chasing the magic number is chasing an illusion, because it not only puts us outside of ourselves and our process, it puts us outside of today—far into the future, where we are free to make up stories based on nothing but fantasy.

There's no such thing as a magic number. But there is such a thing as magic. What feels like magic is different for all of us—a bluebird on the windowsill, a beautiful sunset, the handmade valentine from our child, the friend who holds our hand and listens to us with compassion and total acceptance—this is true prosperity. And true prosperity always feels like magic. Because it is.

"Money is a means to an end, not the end itself."
—EDWENE GAINES

WHAT IS ENOUGH?

The prosperous heart is abundant. While we may not have all that we wish, we can be assured that we have "enough." Rather than insatiably craving more, the prosperous heart makes the most of the stores that it has. We find we can meet our needs and even our wants. We know that prosperity is more than our cash flow, more than our fiscal bottom line. Prosperity is a matter of faith. The prosperous heart trusts that the future will be cared for, as is the day at hand. The prosperous heart does not fear abandonment. It claims God as its constant companion. There is one prayer it prays above all: "Thy will be done." Setting aside its personal will, it asks for knowledge of God's will and the power to carry it out. This prayer is answered, sometimes boldly, sometimes subtly. The prosperous heart believes that even its tiniest whisper meets God's ear.

Andrea was a millionaire. Deeply spiritual, she considered herself truly blessed. She had achieved her magic number and beyond. She had work she passionately loved, for which she was handsomely paid. She planned to use a good portion of her fortune for charity; just as soon as she had "enough" extra, she would make her endowments. In the meanwhile, her investments were yielding a high return—at least, that was what her broker said.

Although she was wealthy, Andrea wanted to be wealthier. Her broker encouraged her to take risks, telling her that her money was safe in his hands. But it wasn't. One horrifying day, Andrea learned that her fortune had been mishandled. She was one of many people who lost their fortune with Bernie Madoff. Rather than investing her money, he had spent it. As her house of cards came crashing down, Andrea found she had a scant $10,000 to her name.

"How could this happen?" she wailed. "I shouldn't have been so trusting. And God should have warned me." Andrea's faith was shaken. In the light of her new situation, she saw her earlier behav-

"Very often people don't so much doubt their guidance as their ability to follow it. This is where friends, the right kind of friends, come in. 'Trust yourself,' these friends say. 'Try it and see what happens. Maybe your guidance is right.'"

—SONIA CHOQUETTE

iors as having been greedy. If she hadn't been trying so hard to have "more," she might have shared the fortune she had accumulated. She felt the sting not only of her own deprivation, but of the needs of the people she would have helped.

"God, how can you have let this happen to me?" she prayed. But she received no answer. For weeks, she thought constantly about her loss, unable to see where it was pointing her. As she started working with the tools, she found herself focusing not on her loss, but on what remained to her. She didn't have a lot, but she had enough.

"I realize I'm still privileged, even without the cushion of my investments. I still work, I can maintain my lifestyle, and as for my dream of helping people—maybe I have more to offer than money."

As Andrea explored her philanthropic ambitions, she was led to found a nonprofit organization with a five-year plan to build ten libraries in impoverished communities. She works tirelessly, and is now well on her way to accomplishing her goal.

"I think God wanted me much more involved," Andrea says with a laugh. "Looking back, I'm ashamed that I ever assumed He just wanted me to write a check. Losing all of my money led me to the most satisfying work of my life. It never occurred to me that I could be the visionary behind this kind of endeavor. I had enough to give after all—and I'm having so much fun."

The prosperous heart feels abundant. This is due to our spiritual, not our fiscal, condition. We know we have what we need. We may even have more than what we need. Sourced by God, we have infinite supply. We find God meets our needs and furthermore may meet our wants. We have been praying for knowledge of God's will and the power to carry it out. Now we find that our prayer has been answered—and that sometimes, God's ideas are even better than our own. We find that our will and God's will are no longer at opposite ends of the table.

WEEK TWO CHECK-IN

Morning Pages: Did you do them this week? How many days?

Counting: Did you count this week? What did you learn?

Abstinence: Did you abstain from debting this week? If you did debt, what was it for? How did you feel?

Walking: Did you walk this week? What insights did you have?

Time-Out: Did you take your Time-Outs? What did you learn?

Prosperity Points

1. Take pen in hand. List three situations about which you could worry. After each entry, tell yourself, "God's got it." *Examples:*
   1. The squabbling and backbiting of our new buyers. (God's got it.)
   2. The cash flow over the summer. (God's got it.)
   3. The meeting with the boss to see about a raise on the next project. (God's got it.)

2. In your journal, number from one all the way to twenty-five. List twenty-five things you absolutely love. When was the last time you were around each one of those items or did each one of those activities? It had been years since I had enjoyed sage and piñon. I lived in New York, but my heart was clearly still in New Mexico. Moving to Santa Fe, I found myself living my list of loves. If you are hesitant to begin, don't worry; most people do not move across the country by the time they are finished making

their list. They do, however, begin to shift into alignment with their true values and, in doing so, develop a more prosperous heart.

3. List three times you have experienced loss, only to discover that it was really gain. The more heightened the emotions, the better. Write them down.

4. What feels like true magic to you? Hint: it costs nothing, you have already experienced it, and it could happen again today. List ten examples from your life.

5. Number from one to five. List five arenas in which you have "enough." This exercise trains you to appreciate abundance.
   Example:
   1. My car. It's not a Mercedes, but it is a solid four-wheel drive and we do have snow.
   2. My furniture. My leather couches have held up well for over a decade.
   3. My food. My neighborhood restaurant features excellent cucumber yogurt soup. I never tire of it.
   4. *Etc.*
   5. *Etc.*

6. List five things you would like to do, but that you tell yourself you do not have enough cash to bankroll. Next to each of your answers, think of one small positive action you could take without spending money.

TRUSTING

By now you may be starting to suspect that there is a benevolent Something that does indeed want you to have a prosperous heart. This week you will explore the idea that you are not alone with your money problems—and that you are safe to have faith in a Higher Power, in yourself, in your ability to handle your finances, and in your dreams. You will look back over your life, noting times when something greater than yourself seemed to have been there for you. Creativity is an act of faith. Identifying your dreams, you will move into action. You have established the groundwork now to trust, and with this newfound courage, you can leap—and know that the net will appear.

THE BENEVOLENT UNIVERSE

I am in New York to teach a workshop, and it is a chill, gray day. Manhattan is socked in. Yesterday had sunshine and high spirits. Today threatens rain. Prudent New Yorkers walk with an umbrella tucked under one arm. They are prepared for the worst. As people walk their dogs, passersby hurry past. No one stops to croon "hello." The dogs are puzzled at being ignored. They wag their gay tails in vain.

"Oh, come on," I can almost hear them thinking. "It's not raining yet."

The dogs have the trick of living in the moment.

The humans rushing past ignore the moment that they are in, dreading the moment that is coming. After all, the weather report tells us it will rain. And it may, but it is not raining now. Now, the sun is playing peekaboo. An optimist might even say the day is turning "nice." But we are not tutored in optimism. We are tutored in dread. We are trained by the media to brace ourselves against impending doom. We are taught to live in apprehension. For many of us, worry is a habit. Worry about money is the most deeply grooved worry of all.

We do not feel we have "enough." No matter how much we have, we want more. We tell ourselves that more is the answer. But is it? Prosperity is spiritual, not fiscal. We can have plenty and still not feel that we have enough.

"Put a little something aside for a rainy day," we are taught. Financial woes are the cloud on our horizon. Just like "bad" weather, fiscal insecurity is bound to come. Our hearts are clenched against the disaster we fear is looming. We may have enough for today, but what about tomorrow? Is our job secure? Have we invested wisely? What if? What if . . . ?

We are in hard times, we tell ourselves. The market is unstable. Insurance is costly. The unemployment rate is high. Even if our investments are stable, our insurance paid for, and our job secure, we are uneasy. It could all change tomorrow, we tell ourselves. And so we dread each day as it unfolds. "Money is tight," we say, feeling the pinch, rehearsing catastrophe. "Times are hard."

We read the papers, searching for a granule of hope.

The news is bad news. We read about scams and frauds. We read of innocent people losing their life savings. We read about deserving workers out of work. Where is there help we can trust? What if we make a poor choice? There is no place for mistakes. One wrong step and . . .

"My life is an adventure. I know that wonderful things are going to happen to me."

—Ernest Holmes

Our minds whirl. Frightened, we find it hard to think clearly. And, we tell ourselves, we must think clearly. If we don't, all will be lost. By "all" we mean that we will lose the house, the job, education for our children, and anything else that we value. We will look like fools, scrambling to pay bills that were once well within our means. And, we tell ourselves, if we have made it okay so far, that is just "so far." Impending doom is sure to come.

But wait.

What if our fearful perceptions are wrong? We *have* been okay so far and we may yet be okay. God willing and the creek don't rise—and God *is* willing—we will be fine. Even if the creek does rise, we will muddle through. "Perhaps," we say to ourselves, "but it would take an act of God."

Yes. And acts of God are beyond number when we are in dire straits. Although we seldom realize it, we can count on them.

Instead, consumed with worry about holding on to what we have, we seldom think of God's helping hand. We may even be mad at God, blaming God for our predicament. Worse still, we may believe that God is mad at us. Our financial difficulties are God's punishment for who knows what. Like Job, we try to have faith. And as our difficulties pile up, we wonder at God's seeming cruelty. "Earn more; spend less," we lecture ourselves, only to have a new and necessary expenditure rear its head. The car gets a flat. The dog needs to go to the vet. We get a notice that we're overdue for our yearly checkup, and without the checkup we cannot renew our prescriptions. We need the prescriptions.

"It is all hosannah. It is all prayer. Jerusalem is walking in this world. Jerusalem is walking in this world."

—Julia Cameron

"I believe in God. I just don't believe that God does money," a friend of mine asserts. "Money" is worldly and God is otherworldly, her belief system goes. When she has financial difficulties, she blames herself. "I should have seen this coming," she scolds herself. God may have started the whole shebang, but after that initial spark it was up to us to run the show. And if times are hard, that proves we've botched it. We're embarrassed in front of our fellows and we are embarrassed in front of God.

We feel a sense of shame around our monetary position. We seek to solve our fiscal predicament by getting smarter. Where can a corner be cut? Where can a bill be delayed? Being broke is our dirty little secret. We do not say, "God, help me"; we do not trust that God will be inclined to help. We may not even trust that God will be savvy enough to know what to do. Instead, we count God out. Worse yet, we develop a resentment. Our financial predicament is God's doing, we decide.

God never gives us more than we can handle, we are told. But we wonder: "Just how much stress does God think I can take?"

"In God We Trust," declares the dollar bill, but we do not take this to heart. We trust the dollar itself, not God. We forget that it is God who provides us with the trust fund we need to meet any circumstance.

When dollars run short, we face the future with fear. We strive to keep our heads above water. We strive to meet our bills and not go further into debt. We strive, period. Life becomes an exercise in apprehension. Some of us stop sleeping. Others of us take to our beds, seeking oblivion. If anyone asks how we are doing, we manage to say, "Fine," or "Okay, thanks." We do not say, "Frankly, I am terrified."

But, frankly, we are terrified.

A friend of mine has achieved—and lost—three fortunes. As he puts it, "When I had lots of dough, I was constantly afraid of losing it. I was never satisfied, never comfortable. There was no magic number that was truly enough. When I was rich, I never thought less about money. I thought about it more."

To the outward eye, this man was prosperous. He made more money than the rest of us and he had the knack of making more still. But the more-money knack only led him into anxiety. Prosperous on paper, he did not have a prosperous heart, a heart that whispered to him, "This is enough; you are enough." Driven to earn and to spend, he tried to buy his way to happiness. He craved the trappings of success. With each status symbol he acquired he had one more thing to lose. Designer clothes, a classy automobile, a chic address—these things bespoke a prosperity he didn't feel. He lost them all.

Spending freely, he overspent. He squandered his wealth, telling himself that each new purchase would turn the trick. A millionaire, he spent like a billionaire. He made money hand over fist, but dollars ran through his fingers. Each time he went broke, he rallied to earn again. With each new fortune, he repeated his prodigal patterns. The one thing he learned was that he never learned. Time and again, he used things to medicate his unease. His heart had a "God-size" hole that could not be filled with cash and prizes. Comparing himself to others, he came up short—and he compared himself to others habitually. His was a life of private misery. Each time he acquired more, he wanted even more than that. He dwelled on his shortcomings and mistakes. "If only I hadn't . . ." he told himself. But he had.

The prosperous heart does not worship money. The prosperous heart is not needy. The prosperous heart asks for—and receives—the blessing of wisdom. Rather than act with fear-driven, shortsighted urgency, we take the longer view, knowing that God is working out events in our favor. Exercising a gentle vigilance, we do not take the superficial view that invites us to proclaim catastrophe. Instead we declare that every circumstance is a God-given opportunity to work things through for the best. God has our best interests at heart. Like the New York City dog that wags its tail on a rainy day, we know this.

"It is within my power either to serve God or not to serve him. Serving him, I add to my own good and the good of the whole world. Not serving him, I forfeit my own good and deprive the world of that good, which was in my power to create."
—LEO TOLSTOY

OUR CREATIVE DREAMS

Exercising our creativity is an act of faith. On every level, in every situation, the act of making something where something did not exist before is in many ways the very definition of faith. Whether we are creating a sculpture, a short story, a proposal for a new project at work, or a dinner party for our friends, the process is the same. We dare to imagine what *could* be—and, trusting our vision, we take steps toward realizing it. We must simply move ahead, doing one "next right thing" after another. This is how all art is made.

Focused on the result, we find it easy to forget that the process of creating *anything* is done a step at a time. Obsessed with how much money our idea might be worth, we find it hard to remember that unless we begin work on the idea, it probably isn't worth much. We must simply begin, and trust that the steps we take, however small, are indeed moving us ahead.

The first step toward accomplishing any creative goal is always doable, and often simple. We assume that to make a movie we need to move to L.A., get an agent, attach a star, raise millions of dollars. But when we approach it this way, we are unlikely to begin at all. Each step seems impossible. We *like* living in Milwaukee. We don't want to leave our family and friends and go to L.A., where we don't know anyone. We don't know any agents, we don't have access to millions of dollars, and we don't have Meryl Streep's number. So we can't begin, then, can we?

Of course we can. The first step is not dramatic. It is not out of our reach. If we have never made a movie, we can start by watching movies in the genre we are attracted to. We can take a filmmaking class at the local college. We can read books on the process. We can search out people in our community who have made movies before, or who know someone who has. We can ask for advice. And a screenplay is written a page at a time, a word at a time, wherever

> "Our challenge and our goal is not to try to fight and manipulate a universe that wants to withhold our good. Instead, it is to accept that the good is here and to give ourselves permission to receive it."
>
> —EDWENE GAINES

we are. A screenplay can be written on our porch in Milwaukee just as easily as—and possibly more easily than—on a beach in L.A.

Appreciating the work of artists who inspire us can go a long way toward expanding our own faith. "Look!" their body of work exclaims. "I kept going! I made something else!"

Peter was a college student in Chicago. Interested in studying architecture, he found himself frustrated by just looking at photographs in books and studying architecture "in theory." One free Saturday, he decided to explore what living inspiration was available to him within his community and within his budget. Taking the train to Oak Park, Illinois, he joined a guided tour of the extensive and breathtaking work of Frank Lloyd Wright. "This is the building he was working on when he died," the tour guide pointed out. "I hope I am always working on a new project—until the day I die," Peter found himself thinking. He returned to his studies excited. The theory, history and technique of architecture were more interesting and more relevant when he had experienced how a master had applied it all. He felt companioned by Wright's work as he imagined his own. He felt inspired by Wright's faith and stubborn productivity. It fueled his research, his focus and his passion.

Contrary to our mythology, Peter was reminded, as artists, we are never alone.

Little is as inspiring as seeing the faithful actions of others. When we witness the process that all artists must go through in order to create, we realize that we can indeed act on our own passions. Any creative work is made by many small steps. The steps themselves are rarely great leaps. It is the faith to begin that we must cultivate and act upon.

"I know exactly what I need to do," my student Rebecca tells me. "I have an idea for a book. I have been thinking about it for years. I am obsessed with religious history, and have done volumes of research. But I have never started my book. I know I need to just

"We know how to sacrifice ten years for a diploma, and we are willing to work very hard to get a job, a car, a house, and so on. But we have difficulty remembering that we are alive in the present moment, the only moment there is for us to be alive. Every breath we take, every step we make, can be filled with peace, joy and serenity. We need only to be awake, alive in the present moment."

—THICH NHAT HANH

open my laptop, start a new document, and try writing. But somehow I always think of one more thing to do instead, whether it's a little more research or folding the laundry. What is wrong with me?"

Rebecca's story is common. Her passion is clear, but her faith in herself to begin is lacking. She is afraid of misstepping, trapped in a mental cycle of perfectionism.

"You need to begin anyway," I tell her. "Like the Nike ad: 'Just do it.' And if you don't *feel* a sense of faith, you need to act anyway. Act *as if* you have faith. As you move forward, you will feel hope, and it will help you continue."

RISK

Risk is the antidote to fear.

When we step forward in faith, our fears dissolve. There is an old saying that goes, "Fear knocked at the door. Faith answered, and there was no one there." My friend, actress Jane Cecil, is fond of reminding me that we always have a choice between faith and fear. It's up to us to decide which one we take to heart.

"But, Jane," I want to say, "that's too simple!"

And yet, Jane's simplicity calms my heart.

Often, all it takes to move from self-loathing to self-respect is one simple action, "the next right thing." My friend Elberta Honstein has made a lifetime out of small, courageous acts. When her daughter suffered a tumor, Elberta undertook healing her, one brave action at a time. At no point did she give up, declaring it was "just too much." Instead, she risked wholeheartedly.

Comparing my risks to Elberta's risks, I am embarrassed. My risks are "luxury problems," not life-and-death. But I remind myself, as I often remind my students, that risk is an individual matter, and what threatens one person—videotaping an online course, in my case—may not threaten another. No matter what challenge we face, our willingness to take the first small risk makes the next risk easier.

"It will be great. You'll do fine. You certainly know the material." Emma Lively's reassuring voice came over the line. I was worrying about the video shoot we had scheduled for the end of the week, aiming to craft an online Artist's Way course.

"I'm worried I'll look fat. I'm worried my answers will be too brief. I'm worried, period. Keep me in the prayer pot."

"There's nothing to worry about. You'll have plenty of support. We'll be able to reshoot anything that doesn't work," Emma continued calmly.

"What about the light?"

"Tricia's bringing lights."

"What if I get uptight?" I pushed.

"Tyler will make you laugh; he always does."

"What if my makeup isn't good on camera?"

"Jackie's bringing makeup."

"Oh."

"Really. Don't worry," Emma insisted. "Everything is taken care of."

I could hear Emma's mounting frustration that I refused to be soothed. I found myself thinking, "She's young and beautiful. No wonder she's not scared of video." I told myself to focus on being of service, not on my looks. I would be the spokesperson for the Artist's Way. I'd been teaching for twenty-five years. This was just one more venue.

"I've got Elberta praying for me," I told Emma. "And Jennifer and Julie and Jane." I ticked off the list of those I'd asked to intercede for me. All four women were spiritual powerhouses. Not to mention Emma herself.

"Try to have faith," Emma pleaded.

"I'll try," I relented. I thought I heard Emma sigh with relief.

"Look at the birds of the air. They neither sow nor reap nor gather into barns, and yet your heavenly Father feeds them. Are you not of more value than they?"

—MATTHEW 6:26

A week later, Emma arrived in Santa Fe and took me to dinner.

"You're going to be fine," Emma pronounced firmly. She sat across from me at Atrisco, my favorite Southwestern restaurant.

"You're going to be fine, and it's going to be fine," she declared. "Everyone knows exactly what they are doing. We won't let you look bad."

I picked at my green chili stew. Emma ate hers with gusto. She was excited to be in Santa Fe, excited about the impending video shoot. She had invited three collaborators to come help her. Tyler Beattie would direct; Tricia Bobeda would be the videographer; Jackie Capp would do hair, makeup, and flowers. Emma herself would be the producer and interviewer. I still felt I was on the hot seat, and I called in a new round of prayers from Elberta, Jane, Julie, and my daughter, Domenica.

"Pray for me to do okay," I asked them. "Pray for me to be of service."

I told Emma about my nerves.

"You might have fun," she ventured.

"Fun?"

"Yes, fun. You know your material inside out. You might enjoy teaching it."

"That's too much to hope for."

"Oh, I don't think so," Emma replied. She was stubbornly optimistic.

"Do you want to take this home?" the waitress asked, indicating my barely touched stew.

"Yes, we will," Emma answered for me. I remembered the guidance I had gotten in my Morning Pages. "Let Emma lead," I had been advised.

"Tomorrow we'll have Jackie do a practice run on your hair and makeup," Emma announced. "For tonight, get a good night's sleep."

Following Emma's marching orders, I turned in early. To my

surprise, I dropped to sleep easily. When I woke up, Emma and Jackie were already on hand. Jackie had an entire suitcase filled with makeup and hair supplies. A fine arts portrait painter, she squinted at me as if at a blank canvas.

"Coffee?" she offered, sensing my apprehension.

"Love some," I agreed.

"Sit here. I'll get it."

I took the indicated chair. Jackie handed me a coffee and then set to work. Her focus was ferocious. She began with a dab of concealer, then a dab of foundation. She used tiny amounts and tiny brushstrokes.

"We want to get rid of the redness," she explained. "Tomorrow I'll use an exfoliant." Slowly, steadily, and carefully she worked on my face. She had studied the fine points of high-definition-video makeup. She explained her techniques as she went along. After an hour's toil, she invited me to look in a mirror. I questioned her brow makeup and she suggested I redo it. I did, and then she worked on my brows some more. She finished my eyes with blue liner and several coats of mascara. I looked in the mirror again and found I looked ten years younger. Jackie finger-combed my hair. It, too, looked more youthful.

"What do you think?" she asked me.

"Excellent," Emma answered for me. "We'll be back tomorrow morning at eight. We'll be quiet setting up locations. You'll be due in the makeup chair at ten. We'll start shooting at noon."

Nervous as I was, I tried to take my cue from Emma. She moved steadily ahead, thinking nothing of driving down to Albuquerque to pick up Tyler and Tricia, who were coming in on late-night flights. Considering all the variables—missed connections, delayed flights—I was immediately nervous. Not Emma. She had faith it would all work out, and her faith was rewarded. By midnight, she and her crew were back in Santa Fe, turning in for the night. I, meanwhile,

"You can open your mind to prosperity by giving up that ridiculous idea that poverty is a Christian virtue, when it is nothing but a common vice."
—CATHERINE PONDER

rotisseried in anxiety. I went to bed early but had trouble falling asleep. I tried to remember Emma's optimism. Finally, I slept.

True to Emma's word, she and the crew arrived at the house at eight a.m. Tricia came laden with equipment. Jackie lugged her suitcase of beautifying brushes, pencils, and potions. Tyler, like Emma, brought optimism. I woke at nine forty-five, just in time to be in the makeup chair by ten.

"Let's start with the basic tools," Emma proposed to me. "We'll record the introduction later, after you're warmed up."

Jackie declared me "done" and "camera ready." I took my place and waited for the camera to roll.

"Ready?" Tyler asked.

"Ready." I nodded.

I began by teaching Morning Pages and Artist Dates. Emma was right that I knew my material inside out. I began to relax. From the basic tools we moved on into "Week One: Recovering a Sense of Safety." Emma cued me with a quote and then we were off and running. "Week One" went smoothly. I didn't ask to see the playback. I decided to trust the team. Jackie hovered nearby, ready to dust me with powder if my makeup started to shine. Tyler listened thoughtfully, prompting me with a specific question between takes. "Yes, awesome," Emma whispered to him excitedly.

Tricia watched from behind the camera, a friendly audience to whom I spoke. We were satisfied with what we got. Emma was ready to move on to "Week Two: Recovering a Sense of Identity." One more time, she cued me to start. I found her cues easy to follow. Our years of working together gave both of us ease with the material. Emma knew the often-asked questions from my students. She cued me to answer them, and as I did, I felt my confidence growing. As Emma had predicted, I started to enjoy myself. I felt a sense of accomplishment as the weekly lessons ticked past.

"I'm actually having fun," I admitted.

"I told you so," Emma gloated. She herself clearly enjoyed her role as producer. Her cues were excellent. We moved smoothly and steadily through the book. At week seven, we stopped for the day.

I found myself tired but jubilant. Emma and her crew went out to celebrate. I put myself to bed, this time less anxious. I slept soundly and woke up early.

The next morning I was eager to get started. Jackie was fussing over floral arrangements. She had a magic touch. Watching her work, I thought, "She's an artist to her fingertips." Flowers finished, she turned her attention to me. She worked quickly and confidently. Makeup and hair took only half of our allotted hour.

"Ready to roll?" Tricia asked.

"Ready," I confirmed.

"Ready," said Emma.

"Roll camera," Tyler announced. Emma fed me a cue and we began filming. Weeks seven, eight and nine went smoothly. "Week Ten: Recovering a Sense of Self-Protection" was challenging. I was getting tired, and the week's lesson was complex and daunting. Emma spoon-fed me her cues. I listened carefully and answered her with care.

"Dear God, please help me here," I prayed to myself. The prayer was answered as we finished the week with a flourish.

"Do you want to rest?" Tyler asked.

"Let's take five," I answered.

"Have you tried the popcorn?" Tricia asked. She had brought four varieties of popcorn with her from Michigan. I crossed to the dining room table, which Emma and Tyler had laden with treats. I helped myself to curried popcorn while Tyler made me a big bowl of fruit salad and granola, sprinkled with balsamic vinegar. It proved to be delicious. Emma gave me a large mug of chai tea. I felt thoroughly refueled and ready to go.

"Week Eleven: Recovering a Sense of Autonomy" unfurled

"If there is disorder or lack of system in your home, overcome it. Affirm: I will be orderly. . . ."
—CHARLES FILLMORE

smoothly. "Week Twelve" also came off without a hitch. All that remained was the introduction. I was worried about it. Emma picked up on my anxiety.

"Don't worry, Julia," she said.

"Are you ready?" asked Tyler, grinning at me.

"I'll try," I answered.

Emma gently cued me and I felt a surge of energy. With ease and aplomb I delivered an introduction.

"Brava, Julia!" Emma exclaimed.

"That's it?" I asked.

"That's it," answered Tyler.

The prosperous heart is tuned to receiving good. It expects the best. Working on the video, Emma displayed a prosperous heart. My own faith was shakier, but the prosperous heart is contagious and, as we worked, I felt my faith strengthening. By video's end, I, too, had a prosperous heart.

In the face of risk, the prosperous heart tutors us in optimism. Looking to the future, it anticipates good. Where the anxious heart feels dread, the prosperous heart feels hope. This hope is grounded in trust. We recognize the many ways God has come through for us in the past. This recognition gives us a foundation. We have a frame of reference that tells us God will provide—and God does provide.

Listing the many ways that God has helped us to prosper leads to an ongoing belief in prosperity. Focusing on the positive, we come to expect further positives. Conversely, if we focus on the negative, we will find ourselves anticipating negativity. The choice is up to us which way we want to view our reality. Our glass can be seen as half full or half empty. If we choose optimism and see our glass as half full, we will very soon see it as brimming over with goodness.

GRATITUDE

A prayer of gratitude is a prayer of celebration. We count our blessings. Rather than pray in entreaty, "Guide me and guard me," we pray with conviction, "I am guided and guarded." We do not need to beg for our good; we need only notice it, accept it and affirm it. We might pray, "Thank you for my serenity," rather than, "Please grant me serenity." Affirmative prayers assume our requests are *already* fulfilled. Affirmative prayers assume our right to a divine dowry. We stake our claim as the beloved child of the universe. Of course God will gift us with, "Yes."

And so we pray prayers of gratitude: "Thank you for finding me the perfect apartment." We claim a good future as if it were unfolding in the present: "Thank you for giving me what I have asked for." Praying affirmatively, the heart experiences a calm sense of abundance. Affirmative prayer forges a link to the Great Creator. We experience God's generosity. There is enough, more than enough, we realize. Our hearts set aside anxiety. We are encouraged, and possessed of a prosperous heart.

At first, the tone of affirmative prayer may feel shocking, hubristic, even sacrilegious. We have been trained to grovel before God. Prayers of petition are what most of us think of when we think of prayer. "Please give me _____." We have been taught to pray to God as to a celestial Santa Claus.

Instead, we need to learn to "ask, believe, receive"—the shorthand for affirmative prayer. A positive outcome is assured; we need only assume that it is so. It takes practice to gain ease and comfort with affirmative prayers. For many of us, affirmative prayer is a radical act, presuming as it does that we are on good footing with God. "Thank you for your guidance," we pray, positing the fact that we are, in fact, guided. "Thank you for your abundance," we pray, when before we had doubt. As we pray affirmatively, we find our

"You are always responsible for the way you accept things that happen to you. . . . [A]ll that really counts is what is happening within you. . . ."
—ERIC BUTTERWORTH

faith broadens and deepens. Eventually, we feel a calm confidence that God hears and answers our prayers.

Instead of petitioning God for some future favor, we thank God for action in the very moment at hand. We pray, "Thank you for your blessings," rather than, "Please bless me." We claim God's goodness in the absolute "now."

"I allow myself to prosper."
—Patricia Bass

The prosperous heart proclaims God's companionship—not in the future once it has been "earned," but in each moment as it is unfolding. "Thank you for your companionship," we might pray. It is a prayer of quiet celebration. God is with us and within us even before we ask. In fact, we need not ask for God's company; instead, we affirm it. "God is within me; I am within God," we may find ourselves declaring. Each time we pray affirmatively we find our sense of oneness with the universe strengthens. We come to know there is one divine presence running through all of life. We take the time to notice and salute the sacred spark within all of life. We are respectful, honoring the holy within every bit of creation. This attitude brings to us a sense of dignity. If all of life is cherished, it is all cherishable, ourselves included. We begin to find ourselves worthy. We experience grace.

The prosperous heart is grateful. Practicing a gentle discipline, we count our blessings and find them numerous, too numerous to name, although we try. To the prosperous heart, every circumstance bears the inky fingerprint of God. If we will accept each situation exactly as it unfolds, we will find in it a hidden blessing. The worst of times contains our best interests. Even in times of hardship, we can find joy.

When we are possessed of a prosperous heart, we do not act out of anxiety. We respond rather than merely react. Doing so, we find our lives filled with choices—and with choices come opportunity. We find every adversity has a silver lining. We are grateful for what we have and we count our blessings. As we focus on them, they seem to multiply. We are grateful for things large and small. We have gratitude for our health and gratitude for our cozy blanket. We have gratitude for our job even as we perhaps search for a better one. Each day unfolds as a gift. We build daily on a solid foundation of appreciation. Comparing ourselves to ourselves alone, we track a gentle and steady improvement.

WEEK THREE CHECK-IN

Morning Pages: Did you do them this week? How many days?

Counting: Did you count this week? What did you learn?

Abstinence: Did you abstain from debting this week? If you did debt, what was it for? How did you feel?

Walking: Did you walk this week? What insights did you have?

Time-Out: Did you take your Time-Outs? What did you learn?

Prosperity Points

1. Ours is a benevolent universe. But when we lack faith, it is hard to believe that we are indeed being guarded and guided. To see that we are safe today, it is helpful to look to the past, noting where God—or the benevolent universe—has stepped in on our behalf. You need not call this Higher Power God. Simply look back over your life and list five times when "an act of God" *could* be the explanation for what came to pass.

Example:

1. It could have been an act of God when I was driving through Texas and was suddenly blinded by the sun—I

was able to pull over to the side of the highway just before a semi passed me at seventy-five mph.

2. It could have been an act of God when Tyler had the sudden vision for how I could take my teaching online—after one evening of impromptu discussion about it, I have now built a new teaching arena.

3. It could have been an act of God when . . .

2. When have you explored a passion fully? Name one passionate interest. Now name another person who has also explored an interest passionately. What did this person teach you? Inspire you to do? Acting in faith, you will inspire others as well.

3. Number from one to three. List three circumstances in which you have taken a risk.

1. Moving to Santa Fe.

2. Speaking honestly with Sarah.

3. Sending my plays to a theater agent.

Now look back at your list and think about what happened when you took these risks. Did God indeed "cover your bet"? In the cases where God did, was your attitude any different than in the cases where God apparently let you down? And did God *actually* let you down, or did the experience end up teaching a valuable lesson? It often does.

1. Moving to Santa Fe, I found myself quickly surrounded by new friends, easily finding a cozy house, and delighted every day by the nature and scenery.

2. When I explained to Sarah that I would need to start paying her biweekly instead of weekly, as she was used to, she was understanding and seemed relieved that I felt comfortable being honest about finances with her.

3. The agent rejected my submission, but having sent my plays out once gave me the courage to do it again. The fourth agent I contacted took me on as a client.

4. Take pen in hand and number from one to ten. List ten things, great or small, for which you are grateful.
   1. My good health.
   2. My sunny apartment.
   3. My dependable car.
   4. My affectionate dog.
   5. My loyal friends.
      Etc.
   Gratitude is a learned skill. Add to your gratitude list daily. At first you may feel hard-pressed to come up with ten items. As you make gratitude a daily practice, more and more items will spring to mind. Before long, you will be able to enumerate twenty-five items instead of ten. As gratitude becomes a habit, so will happiness. The prosperous heart is a happy heart. Like gratitude, happiness is a habit—a choice we can trust ourselves to make.

5. Once again, take pen in hand and now practice affirmative prayer. Choose five issues in your life that you wish were happily resolved, and thank God for resolving them.
   1. God, thank you for your ongoing guidance with this book.
   2. God, thank you for providing an adequate cash flow.
   3. God, thank you for bringing me love and affection.
      Etc.

Week Four

CLEANING HOUSE

Knowing that you are partnered by a Higher Power, you are now emboldened to step back into your immediate surroundings and take a personal inventory, past and present. You will look at your home and what you surround yourself with on a daily basis. You will remove clutter and clear a physical path to your dreams and desires. You will look at the people you have shared and continue to share yourself and your money with and examine which relationships were and are truly supportive—which ones you would like to strengthen, which ones you might like to let go of.

This week, you will also take a fresh look at your numbers and make the first gentle, calm steps toward getting out of debt. By now you are getting to know your spending patterns, and your spending may have already started to more accurately mirror your values. By cleaning up the past, you will clear a path toward future solvency. This week will take courage and honesty, but have faith: the rewards are well worth it.

CLUTTER

Nothing impedes the flow of money like physical clutter. An environment that is stuffed and jammed with unneeded papers and knickknacks is an environment in which no clear thinking can be accomplished. Without clarity, there is no prosperity. Clearing away the rubble makes for clear thoughts.

Angela lived in a clutter-filled home. She allowed her mail to pile up, and she often misplaced important correspondence. When I suggested to Angela that she try decluttering, she was at first resistant. She found her clutter comforting, like a bird's nest made of this and that. I suggested that she begin by tackling her mail. She set aside two hours to deal with the two towering piles on her kitchen table. She found that most of her mail was offers for credit cards. But two important notices dealt with her insurance. She filled out the forms and mailed them in, just in the nick of time. Also included in her mail was a notice for her high school reunion. Angela took the time to read it, and decided that yes, she would like to go. A third unopened piece of mail was a thank-you note for services rendered, and an offer to help publicize her new business venture. Angela responded to this letter with a letter of her own: yes, she would like the help. By the time an hour and a half had passed, Angela had reached the bottom of the second pile and felt a welcome rush of clarity. She resolved that in the future she would keep her in-box current.

Next, Angela tackled her bedroom. She had mounds of clothes at the foot of her bed. All of the items had been worn once, and were not really dirty. Scooping a pile of hangers from her closet, Angela hung up her clothes. She had been wearing one outfit day in and day out. Now she saw that she had choices, and her bedroom looked welcoming for the first time in months. Her bathroom came next. Angela had bottles and potions balanced on the edge of her sink. Carefully, she recapped them and put them in her medicine cabinet. All that remained out was a cleansing lotion she actually used. Finally, it was back to the living room. The coffee table was stacked with unread magazines. Rather than tell herself, "I'll get to

"Prosperity is the consciousness of God present everywhere."
—EDWENE GAINES

them," Angela tossed them into the recycling bin. As she started to free up space, her house began to feel habitable for the first time. She realized that many of her belongings were pretty, and she felt gratitude for her abundance, previously unnoticed.

Taking a tablet and a pen, she curled up on the sofa in the corner and made a list of actions she could take to further her prosperity. To her surprise, ten actions came to her. Clearing away the rubble had allowed her to think clearly. Clearing clutter is a homely action, yet a bold one. Setting to work, we tackle one room—or even one corner of a room—at a time. A kitchen may feature crowded cabinets and an overstuffed refrigerator filled with out-of-date foods. Tossing out the foods with expired dates makes way for new, fresh foods and the sense of self-worth that comes from taking care of ourselves. The bathroom filled with clutter is not serene. As we put away or discard bottles and potions, we create an inviting environment in which we can experience a healthy sexuality. We are desirable, we realize. Our bedroom is another arena for clutter to congregate. We may be leaving the bed unmade or shedding our clothes in a pile. Hanging up our clothes leaves us with an inviting bed where we can enjoy a good night's rest. Often our living rooms are cluttered with unread magazines, dishes from hurried meals, and empty soda pop cans. Clearing away this litter transforms our lair into a hospitable home. Our dining room or kitchen table often becomes the "mail dump." Mounds of mail accumulate without our surveillance. Unwashed dishes in the sink distract us each time we pass them. But all it takes is a modest commitment in time and energy to open our correspondence and respond, to load the dishes into the dishwasher. The effort is small; the rewards are large.

Taylor was an esteemed college professor who taught at an Ivy League school. Widely regarded as a genius, he had published several books and was sought after in educational circles. But Taylor's office and classroom were notoriously messy, becoming a joke among the students and faculty. Good-natured and unembarrassed, Taylor tolerated the jesting, continued to teach beautifully, and let his office and classroom get messier by the year. When the college began a search for a new president, the dean of the school sent a message to the faculty, letting them know that they should be prepared to have the potential new boss stop by to see their work at any time, and the dean hoped that everyone would "be prepared in every way" for a visit. Taylor suspected that the dean would directly approach him about the state of his office and classroom next, and so he began decluttering for the first time in years. Two days and twelve trash bags later, Taylor was elated. He called his wife, Irma, who, upon seeing the uncovered rooms, burst into laughter and started taking pictures.

When Irma sent the pictures to her friend Katherine, expecting that Katherine, too, would find them hilarious and delightful, Katherine called immediately. To Irma's surprise, Katherine was earnest. "Be very gentle with him," Katherine whispered. "He's had an epiphany."

Following Katherine's advice, Irma watched Taylor carefully. Sensing a sadness in him, she prodded him gently. "I feel so guilty," Taylor said. "I realize now that although I thought I was 'getting away with it'—even calling my messiness my absentminded professor 'brand,' I actually was treating my students—and myself—with less respect than we all deserve. So many of my students have commented that they can concentrate better in my classroom now. There's nothing I care about more than their education, and I see that I was being careless by letting the learning environment be distracting. Just because I *can* concentrate amid clutter doesn't mean that I should—or that other people should be forced to. And I actually concentrate much better when things are in order, too." Call it an epiphany; call it a spiritual awakening; call it what you like— Taylor's shift was practically on a cellular level. For the first time, his surroundings accurately reflected his brilliance.

"I acknowledge and declare that the Creator of all things is now manifesting as perfection and harmony in all my experiences."
—Ernest Holmes

There are several ways we can ease into our own process of decluttering. First, buy a large box of trash bags, preferably the type with a drawstring. Next, set a timer for fifteen minutes. Working as fast as you can, charge through the house, throwing away anything unneeded, unused, unwanted. Set the timer again, and do a second fifteen minutes. Repeat fifteen-minute intervals for an hour. Most houses can be decluttered on the surface within an hour's time—and the surface is a great place to start. Any progress—even superficial progress—will inspire more. If your house is one that will take more than an hour, be gentle with yourself and don't rush. Put in an hour a day until you are clean and clear. We are after progress here, not perfection. Paperwork and filing can take time. Decluttering closets filled with old and unused clothes can take time. The point is to do it in small chunks of time. Fifteen minutes of progress at a time is enough.

The prosperous heart is free. It is not distracted or weighed down by baggage and clutter. As we declutter our homes, we make room for our true dreams to grow.

A MONEY HISTORY

As your physical environment becomes clearer, your mind becomes clearer, as well. Getting rid of physical clutter lightens your psyche, allowing room for your thoughts to process. At this point in the course you are "cleared," and thus ready to do a difficult exercise, but one that will bring great reward. You will now look at the *people* who have historically cluttered your financial life. Certain people may immediately come to mind: those who have been generous with you, those who have not. You may suspect that it is time for certain relationships to be addressed. You are correct.

This week, you will be writing a Money Autobiography. Working in five-year increments, allow yourself to recall what your cash flow was, where it came from, and where it went. Who were the major players in your life, and how did they impact your finances? Did you make loans? Did you buy extravagant gifts? Were you a miser, hoarding your cash? Jot down "cues" that help you to remember. You're not writing a novel. You're not writing a dissertation. You're simply outlining your money behaviors.

Do not be frightened by this exercise. You are asked merely to list and not to judge. Start at age zero. Did you receive an allowance as a child? What did you spend it on? If it was candy, do you have a lingering sweet tooth? What about babysitting money? Did you spend it all on entertainment? Did you save up for a purchase of something you really valued? Did you take loans for college? When you got your first grown-up job, did you save or spend? Charting our Money History moves us toward monetary health. Prosperity does not exist in denial.

Deirdre discovered that she had a pattern of overspending other people's money. It began in childhood, when her father spoiled her, giving her money to buy whatever she wanted. By college, she had a pattern of finding rich friends who would spend on her behalf. By the time she married, she chose a free-spending older man. His money was her money. She wanted to be a movie producer, and her husband bankrolled her dreams. Soon, however, his cash flow was not enough for her. She tapped her wealthy friends to invest in her schemes. Before long, she had run through millions—monies not her own, but to which she felt entitled. When her free-spending husband wound up in jail, Deirdre had to manage her own financial future for the first time. She started by examining her past.

"In a dark time, the eye begins to see."
—Theodore Roethke

"I spent everybody's money as if it were my own. I lived high on the hog. By calling other people's money 'investments' rather than 'loans,' I was able to justify *everything*." Deirdre felt a substantial shock at this point. "No more borrowing. No more 'investing,'" she pledged to herself. At age fifty-five, she was not too old to change her money pattern, using the triple *As*: Awareness, Acceptance, Action.

There are three stages that we must pass through in attaining financial stability. Awareness comes to us through Counting. Prosperity begins with clarity. No longer unconscious, our money behaviors are there for us to see in black and white. This is the first step.

The second step, our Monetary Autobiography, moves us into acceptance. We see our long-standing patterns and we accept responsibility. For many of us, our money patterns come as a substantial jolt. But that jolt is often followed by a sigh of relief. At last, we see the script we have been living out. For many of us, our spending, borrowing, and loaning habits have their roots in childhood. And so, it is time for compassion—for ourselves and others.

As we move into action, we exercise courage: we step forward into the unknown, moving ahead even when the outcome is uncertain. Action is our power: when we are in action, our lives are in action. We are not stagnant. We are not powerless.

Set aside one hour. This is enough time to write your Money History. You can always go back and fill in further details as they come to you. You may find that some periods are emotionally fraught. Do not dwell on difficult times. Simply note them. You are aiming for detachment. "Just the facts, ma'am, just the facts."

Use the following guidelines to write your Money History. Remember: only an hour.

MY MONEY HISTORY

Ages 0–5

1. I was aware of money when _____

2. I wanted money for _____

"The past is dead. The future is imaginary. Happiness can only be in the Eternal Now Moment."

—KEN KEYES JR.

3. In my household, money was _____

4. I wished that I had _____

5. I received money when _____

Ages 5–10

1. My allowance was _____

2. I earned money for _____

3. I wanted money to _____

4. In my household, money was _____

5. I wished that I had _____

Ages 10–15

1. My allowance was _____

2. I earned money for _____

3. I wanted money to _____

4. In my household, money was _____

5. I wished that I had _____

Ages 15–20

1. My allowance was _____

2. I earned money for _____

3. I wanted money to _____

4. In my household, money was _____

5. I wished that I had _____

Ages 20–present, in five-year increments:

1. I earned money by _____

2. I spent money on _____

3. I saved money for _____

4. I gave money to _____

5. I wasted money on _____

6. I was given money by _____

7. I wanted money to _____

8. I wished I had money to _____

9. I shared my money with _____

10. I thought money would _____

When you have finished your Monetary Autobiography, take yourself for a twenty-minute walk to help you integrate any insights gained during the process.

ANGER

In spite of your achievements, you may find yourself in a less-than-celebratory mood. As you practice not debting, you may move into a new area of recovery called Withdrawal. For many of us, the withdrawal from debting is characterized by the feeling that we are going crazy. In point of fact, we are "going sane," and that feels crazy to us. You slam the door. You snap at your lover for no reason. You storm out of the house because someone didn't fold the laundry. What's going on? Anger. Why? Withdrawal. For years you have used money—or the lack of it—to block your feelings, and now those blocked feelings are coming out. Often, debt masks our rage. Worrying about being evicted, who had time to worry about the fact that no one helped you with the housework? Worried about a phone bill, who had the energy to focus on a friend who never called? Suddenly we want reciprocity, a return to balance, and not just in the checkbook. We want respect, and we want courtesy. We want "please" and "thank you." We are angry at being taken for granted. We've been angry for a long time, but we've been afraid to express it. We've been charming and nice, saying, "It's okay," when it really isn't. We've known that someday, broke, we would need a favor. "Pitch in around here," we suddenly demand of the children we have waited on hand and foot.

We must be careful not to snap at our loved ones at these moments. Our anger is fuel, and it must be used carefully. We are in a process of awakening, and this is not necessarily a graceful process. We must be alert to our emotions and be thoughtful about how we act on them.

As we alter our behaviors toward money, our relationships with those around us alter, too. This is normal. When we are no longer automatically paying for dinner, our friends must step up—or meet us at noncostly destinations where both parties can contribute. Some of our friends may react negatively to our newfound clarity. The good deal they were getting has run out. As we stand firm, we build our bank account *and* our self-worth.

"My life is a life filled with the abundance of God's blessings."
—Unknown

OUT OF DEBT

At this point in the course, you have stopped debting for a prolonged amount of time. This is a triumph worthy of celebration. Although the debt load you are carrying may still overwhelm you, the fact that no new debt has been acquired is worth noting with pride.

Once we've come to an awareness and acceptance of our spending patterns, it is time to take action in terms of our existing debts. Our homes have been cleared of clutter, and our Money History has brought us mental clarity, past and present. Now we must clear our actual debt and the weight it brings on us. Creditors feel free to phone us at all times of day and night. Our homes do not feel safe. We feel harassed, and we *are* harassed, until we take action on our own behalf.

Be gentle but thorough, and make a list of all your debts, personal and business. Pick up the phone and call your creditors. Explain that you are in financial recovery and that you will be paying them soon. Offer them an amount you know you can pay each month. Do not make unrealistic promises. Explain that you *will* pay, but that you must pay at a manageable rate. We are aiming at digging out, not digging further into debt. Most creditors will welcome your goodwill and good intentions. Remember: do not promise more than you can pay. Give yourself a block of time to stabilize your resources. Remember that your creditors have *already* been waiting.

Jeannette began her Abstinence with great anger. She had run herself into debt by making loans to her extravagant loved ones. Their debts to her were never repaid, and her debts to creditors were the result.

"No more loans," she told herself, and, taking phone in hand, she called those creditors who had been calling her. "I'll begin repaying you in a month," she told them. To her surprise, the creditors welcomed her offer. Some of them even offered to lower her interest rate. Jeannette's lover asked her for one last loan. "No," she said, although she worried that a *no* would end her relationship. It did not. Her lover merely laughed nervously and said, "I'll have to go elsewhere, I guess." Jeannette marveled at this turn of events. Saying no to her lover, Jeannette began to say yes to herself. For the first time, she experienced the self-respect that comes from reciprocity, and began to have a prosperous heart.

"I felt adrenaline replacing fear as one by one I called my creditors. When I said no to my lover, I felt my apprehension melting away and self-respect taking its place. I was so excited, I almost went on a shopping spree. I caught myself in the nick of time, and found myself writing in my journal to celebrate my victories."

The paradox of not debting is that we actually experience a prosperous heart when we live within our means. Not debting, we see what we already have, and often see that it is already enough. Communicating with our creditors and making a plan to remove debt from our lives completely, we open the door to a naturally abundant life. We do not need to go into debt to acquire more. Worthy actions on our own behalf create true self-worth. Not borrowing from our future, we are truly free.

WEEK FOUR CHECK-IN

Morning Pages: Did you do them this week? How many days?

Counting: Did you count this week? What did you learn?

Abstinence: Did you abstain from debting this week? If you did debt, what was it for? How did you feel?

Walking: Did you walk this week? What insights did you have?

Time-Out: Did you take your Time-Outs? What did you learn?

Prosperity Points

1. Take pen in hand and list ten actions you could take to keep your home clutter-free going forward.
   1. I could take all the change in the house to the bank and deposit it in my checking account.

2. I could cancel the subscriptions to magazines I don't read.
3. I could donate some books I no longer need to the library.
4. I could invest in a once-a-month housekeeper to help me keep clutter at bay.
5. I could _____

2. Fill in the following sentence ten times:

   1. I am angry that _____

   2. I am angry that _____

   3. I am angry that _____

3. Answer the following questions:
   1. How have you been doing with Counting? What have you learned? Were there arenas in which you overspent? Were there arenas in which you underspent? What did you learn about your values? Did you spend money along authentic lines? What adjustments can you make to your spending pattern? Do you have more money than you thought?
   2. How have you been doing with Abstinence? Is it getting easier not to debt? Have small "miracles" occurred to keep you from debting? Does a debt-free life give you a sense of prosperity? Has your self-worth improved with your Abstinence? Do you feel supported in ways that have surprised you?

   Answering these questions, do you experience optimism? Take a deep breath, take pen in hand, and list your creditors. Pick up the phone.

FINDING COMMUNITY

L ast week you were focused inward as you took an intimate inventory of your physical, emotional, and financial life. This laid important groundwork, and you are stronger for it. This week I urge you to go out into the world and explore the vast opportunities and support available to you—opportunities that you will be able to see, and support you will be able to accept, since you have now cleaned house and made room for good.

You will be looking at your "inner circle," those people who are intimately involved in your day-to-day life. You are ready now—and will be guided—to make adjustments in how you spend your time, money, and energy. You may find yourself setting boundaries and acting with a newfound clarity and sense of self-protection in your personal and financial relationships. You will pursue interests and adventures that truly feed you and begin to explore them. You will find that "to prosper" is an action you can take—and in taking prosperous actions, you will develop a prosperous heart.

THE INNER CIRCLE

All of us have an "inner circle" of friends, family, and people we interact with on a regular basis. As we strive to live prosperously, it is important to look closely at those people who are the major players in our lives. Are they the right players? Are there people whom we wish to be closer to, or more in contact with, than we are? Are there those whom we communicate with daily, only to feel drained or misunderstood after each interaction?

In gently forging our inner circle, we must look for what I call "believing mirrors," those people who reflect back to us our full potential. Believing mirrors are encouraging. They see the best in us. They believe our projects will come to fruition. They trust that it is God's will for us to be creative, for us to be solvent and prosperous.

When I travel between Santa Fe and New York, which I often do, there is no direct flight, and I entertain myself by reading tabloids. Arriving at the airport, I stop at the newsstand. I load up on tabloids and try to ignore the judgment of the cashier as he rings up thirty dollars' worth of gossip. The tabloids change their story lines from week to week: one week is divorce; the next week is reconciliation; the third week is divorce again. Many of the players are unknown to me. The escapades of Kim, Kourtney, and Khloe have never captured my imagination. I do not watch the weekly antics of the "housewives" shows. And yet, I read with empathy about the breakdowns of Britney Spears and the excesses of Lindsay Lohan. There are those who believe the tabloids are unbelievable. My own experience suggests that they are all too true. If the tabloids say a man has a violent temper, I believe them. If a woman has a problem with substance abuse, that, too, rings true.

Even so, why do I read them? Why am I drawn to the stories; why do I feel deep empathy, compassion, interest? Because this world was once where I found my inner circle.

Tabloids take me back thirty years to my own time in Hollywood. It was a dark time, with my marriage on the rocks and Liza Minnelli featured as the other woman. When I read stories of excess and infidelity, I am grateful to be years removed from the scene of the crime. Even the most outrageous stories, like Charlie Sheen's, remind me of the past. I count my blessings to be now many years clean and sober, far from the cocaine madness and marital woes.

In my carry-on, along with the stack of tabloids, I also carry a book entitled *1000 Years of Sobriety.* Published by Hazelden, it contains the stories of twenty sober alcoholics who have logged more than fifty years apiece without a drink. The stories are not well written, but they are compelling. I find myself avidly reading, and drawing comparisons with my own drinking and recovery. A universal theme, story to story, is great gratitude for the miracle of sobriety. I find myself thinking that the book is like an antitabloid— the lurid drinking days eclipsed by the sunny times of sobriety.

The irony of this book juxtaposed with my stack of tabloids is not lost on me. They both represent significant, formative parts of my life—filled with lessons and experiences that were all a part of leading here, to this moment, today. We all have our individual history, our map to our values, to our serenity.

As we define our inner circle, we can discard those who do not play by our rules. Gone are the people who take advantage of our good nature. Gone are the people who always ask for more than their fair share. We can learn from our experiences—the traumatic ones as well as the joyful ones. We can learn to protect ourselves, to fill our lives with people whose values match our own, who bring compassion and humor and kindness with them, who accept our gifts in return.

"Through the act of affirmative prayer the limitless resources of the Spirit are at my command. The power of the Infinite is at my disposal."
—ERNEST HOLMES

AROUND THE DINNER TABLE

A few weeks after moving to Santa Fe, I decided to start a Wednesday-night tradition. I would cook and invite people to dinner. I would play hostess, entertain new guests, listen, and share. I was searching for a new inner circle.

It's three forty-five on a Wednesday afternoon. Dinner guests are arriving at six fifteen. The sweet and savory aromas of pie and roasting chicken fill the house. Tiger Lily, my dog, eddies hopefully in front of the oven. She is ready to eat now. Tonight's dinner is old-fashioned comfort food: roast chicken, rice pilaf, buttermilk biscuits, spinach salad fruit salad and broccoli with pesto, followed up by two pies, one cherry and one berry.

The Wednesday-night meals are becoming a tradition for me and for a growing circle of friends. I find that inviting a sometimes consistent, sometimes changing group of people into my home once a week allows me to build a community in Santa Fe, getting to know my neighbors and colleagues and welcoming these new friends into my world. Good food goes with good conversation. Although tonight's menu features familiar foods, tonight's guests feature a mix of known entities and strangers. I have invited two men about whom I know nothing except that, having met them socially, I like them both. One man is a psychologist, newly retired. I don't know what trade the other man plies.

Dinner will be served at seven, allowing us a half hour for conversation before our meal. This is an innovation. I was serving dinner sharply at six thirty, but I found the meal then felt rushed. With time before and time again between the meal and dessert, the evening should prove more hospitable. I have discovered that I love cooking for my friends.

Cooking a home-style dinner takes me about three to five hours. While the pies are baking, I settle in to write. I get down a rough draft of my thoughts, and then, when the roast is in, I polish what I've done. Last to go in the oven are the biscuits. They take twenty minutes, and I am often pulling them out just as my guests arrive. Rex carves and his wife, Michele, sets out the silverware and dishes.

The finished meal is a casual, collaborative affair. We eat at leisure, dawdling over dessert.

Visitors to my little house note the many Audubon prints that grace the walls. To my great delight, one of my new Santa Fe friends, Rex Oppenheimer, has a brother who is America's leading expert on Audubon. When I cook for Rex, he eats under the watchful eye of a great blue heron. Herons were among my father's favorite birds. I learned to bake pies from my mother. It gives me a sense of abundance and connection to honor my parents in these small ways. They are here at dinner with us in spirit.

At the end of the evening my guests always insist on cleaning up, leaving the kitchen spotless—usually more spotless than it was before I started cooking in the afternoon. My guests are generous, and reciprocity is assumed. I have been invited many times to their houses, as well.

On Christmas Eve, my frequent dinner guests Michele and Rex picked me up and drove me to the tiny village of Galisteo, twenty miles outside of Santa Fe. In Galisteo, we made our way past the Catholic church, which had two enormous bonfires burning out front. A hundred yards farther on, we turned right into the long driveway of Cory's house. A photographer and chef, our hostess for the night lives in an artfully decorated home. As we entered, the scent of tamale pie met our nostrils. Opening the refrigerator to offer us drinks, Cory revealed a large, festive bowl of trifle. "It's lime custard, gingerbread, and macaroons," she explained. "But first, tamale pie."

"You must remember that man is noble, man is sublime, man is divine, and can accomplish whatever he desires."
—Swami Muktananda

Michele set out her offering, a Moroccan dish featuring spinach, garbanzo beans, and couscous. I set my cherry pie to one side. After our international feast, culminating in the British trifle, Cory suggested we go out for a walk.

"Yes! Let's do!" came the enthusiastic response.

Piling into coats and scarves, we followed Cory into the night.

The sky was pitch but the stars were brilliant. The Milky Way sprawled horizon to horizon. The footing was muddy, and I stepped ankle-deep into a puddle. Picking our way through the darkness, we reached the church. The bonfires had become embers. A mass was in process. Not wanting to disturb the mass, our little group headed back the way it had come. This time, we knew to avoid the puddles. Carefully, we made our way through the inky black, our way lit only by starlight.

The prosperous heart has reciprocal relationships. The give-and-take comes out even. The prosperous heart is generous, and its friends are generous in return. The prosperous heart neither overgives nor undergives. It believes in fair play. It offers reciprocity. It is always willing to meet a new friend.

TAKING ACTION

"To prosper" is a verb—and an action we can take.

Yesterday I drove to Taos. I don't know why I did it—Taos is, for me, the scene of many crimes. I often drive in Santa Fe—the New Mexico mountains inspire me daily, with their velvet folds changing color moment by moment. As I approached the familiar Taos terrain for the first time in years, I had an acute desire to turn back. But I found myself driving just a little farther—to the ranch I had lived in during the period I was married, when Domenica was finishing high school and I was writing *The Right to Write.*

Driving up to "my" ranch, I was struck by sadness. The fences were in disrepair. The outbuildings needed paint. The once-beautiful ranch was now a shambles. I remembered the loving care I had given to the property when it was mine. I felt anger at the mess the ranch had fallen into . . . as if it *were* mine. Why did I still feel like it was mine?

"Then the Lord your God will restore your fortunes and have compassion on you."

—Deuteronomy 30:3

Much of the money I earned from the publication of *The Artist's Way* had gone into that house. The trim was still aqua, but the fences were peeling, falling down, the fields dry and overgrown. What was once home now looked like a stranger's abode—and it was. I looked at the crumbling barn and wondered whether my mother's Christmas ornament collection was still hidden in the rafters. I had never found her ornaments again after the move. I saw the windows to the back room where I had allowed an artist friend to live, rent-free, for many years. I looked across the street to the now decrepit Mexican restaurant that Domenica and I "sort of" liked, but frequented regularly, always optimistic.

My feelings were complex. I missed this house, this life, and was at once repelled by it. It represented a time of gain and a time of loss . . . the beginning of a financially prosperous time, and the beginning of a period that would be costly on every level. Taos was a dangerous place for me. I suffered two breakdowns with no doctors on hand. I was later told in no uncertain terms that the New Age suggestions of the locals put my life squarely in danger, and I was lucky to have survived. Indeed.

While I lived here, my finances were in danger, too. Many people spent my money during this period. Accountants who thought my "prayer life was strong"—and so they didn't file my taxes. Lawyers who billed me for services they never rendered. Astrologers who promised to bring me to health using the stars and a piece of amethyst—for only $800 an hour. Fragile, I was sometimes fooled. Desperate, I listened to the party line. And then, as I miraculously returned to health, I became angry. *Very* angry. In a burst of clarity, I left. I fired the accountants and the lawyer. I moved to New York. I found good doctors. I rebuilt my life and restored my finances, one action at a time.

This time, I trusted the right people. My grounded New York friends looked out for me. I hired a new manager, Emma, who

"In order to demonstrate true prosperity, you must get rid of what you do not want, to make way for what you do want."
—CATHERINE PONDER

scoffed at the state of my affairs as they arrived in one jumbled box after another from Taos. "Who did this?" Emma asked. "Who *are* these people?" It took weeks for Emma and two assistants to unpack what had been my office in Taos.

I was living on Seventy-second Street at the time, working on a book in my writing room, when Emma entered one day, holding a box.

"This box is marked 'divorce settlement,'" she said. She held the box out to me. Inside was a broken tape recorder, a children's book, a stapler, some loose change. "This is the tip of the iceberg," she said, her eyes dark. "This will never happen to you again."

Emma and her help restored my office to sanity. In the end, none of the boxes was marked correctly. Each one that was unpacked was a reminder, there in front of my eyes, of the chaos that had been Taos.

And yet, more than a decade later, I returned to the scene of the crime. I sat, parked outside of that ranch, flooded with memories. It was difficult for me to see the house without feeling called to action. How much money would it take? I found myself thinking. I would rehang the gates; I would mend the fences. I would paint the trim with a fresh coat of aqua. But no, I would not. These were not the right actions. I lived there no longer, and I would do best to put the past behind me.

It is always important to look closely at our inner circle. It is especially important to think twice about those who ask to enter it when we have come upon a windfall. When we come into money, it is common for people to come out of the woodwork with their hands out. Optimistic, we don't necessarily have an automatic sense of suspicion. When we are feeling elated and generous, it is easy to give to others without thinking it through. As much as possible, though, when we are suddenly flush, we must take the time to connect with ourselves. When others ask us to share our bounty, "Let me get back to you" is always an appropriate response.

Action involves responsibility. We may have a list of others who we feel have taken advantage of us, but closer examination tells us that we were willing to be taken advantage of. *We* trained others that our money was theirs for the asking. We are the ones who were afraid to say no. We need to practice saying no, to recognize that *no* is the beginning of *yes*—yes to ourselves, yes to the life we choose to lead, yes to prosperity instead of poverty, a prosperous heart instead of an anxious one.

MENTORS

As we look for community, there are few people who are more valuable than mentors. I myself have—and have had—many mentors. Sister Julia Claire, my writing teacher from high school, is still a confidante and teacher of mine. Ninety-two years old, she is as sharp as ever, and can always be relied upon to offer guidance and direction. As a teacher now myself, I see the benefits of being a mentor, as well.

My friend Judy Collins is always learning. A woman who has traveled the world to perform, she has seen many countries and met many people. It seems that each new experience makes her more open than the last. Bright and alert, she is like a bird flitting from one beautiful flower to the next. She is both energetic and serene. A friend of mine says of Judy, "She is so youthful and also so wise. I can't tell whether she seems sixteen years old or five hundred years old!" I agree with my friend. And I suspect Judy's vigor is a byproduct of her openness, and eagerness, to learn.

Judy is constantly reading. She reads about history, about politics, about spirituality. She reads novels and biographies and poetry. She

"In demonstrating prosperity you should praise and bless even minor evidences of financial improvement."
—Charles Fillmore

gives books to her friends when she "can't fit another volume" in her house. Her famous blue eyes light up when she talks about a new author she has happened upon. She is always ready to talk for hours about new discoveries she has made, new things she has learned. A gifted listener, she assumes she has something to learn from everyone she meets. She speaks of how she actively looks for friendship in young people. I'm not surprised. Her energy is much like that of a thirty-year-old. And to the thirty-year-olds in her life, she is both generous with her wisdom and open to theirs.

A mentor to an energetic young songwriting team, Judy laughs with delight when the enthusiastic composers bring her their latest song. "This was inspired by you," they say, handing her a CD. "We wrote a role for you in this show," they say, handing her a script. "This one's dedicated to you." Judy listens with interest to their ideas, sharing her own. As the writers thank her profusely for inspiring them, Judy laughs unassumingly. "Oh, you inspire me back." She smiles. "I'm a fan. That's all."

As we look for people to mentor ourselves, it is important to remember how valuable our words may be to the younger person. Telling someone that we are their "fan," we give them permission to be their biggest, most prosperous self. "You're special," we tell them. "I see you."

Being "seen" is often all we need to inspire us to keep making plans, to keep charging ahead, to keep chasing our dreams. Sharing our inspiration with others continues a positive cycle of prosperity. Our own generosity gifts us as well.

ADVENTURE

Adventure—taking risks, large and small, on our own behalf—both requires and breeds enthusiasm. One of the greatest gifts of prosperity we can give to ourselves is to allow ourselves frivolity and play. Exploring my new home of Santa Fe is a daily adventure. Staying open to new experiences is a daily habit. But even if you have lived in your town for thirty years, new adventures are *always* available if you look for them. In previous books I have recommended taking Artist Dates—weekly solo adventures—to keep yourself fresh and inspired. Artist Dates need not be "high art." They can be a trip to a museum or to a pet store. They can be a walk in the woods, a solo dinner at an exotic restaurant, a concert, a bus tour, a movie. But Artist Dates do not have to be limited to once a week. You can incorporate adventures, big and small, into your everyday life.

A small step toward adventure takes courage, but the reward of increased self-worth is large. Can I do something just for fun? Do I deserve to take an hour "off" to play? Can I afford it? The answer is yes, you do deserve it. And I would argue that you can't afford *not* to. As we venture out into the world, we are put in touch with ourselves, our spirit, a sense of optimism, and a lightness of heart.

My phone rang one morning soon after I'd moved to Santa Fe, and the voice on the other end belonged to Cory. She told me she was working in her friend's silk shop and she wondered if I'd like to drop by.

"Where is it?" I asked.

"Do you know where Borders is?"

"No."

"Do you know where Sanbusco is?"

"No."

"You really need to; it's a fun district, just off Guadalupe."

Getting off the phone, I tried to drop back to sleep, but to no avail. I was awake for good. Padding into the kitchen, I made a pot of coffee. While it brewed, I wrestled up a skillet of bacon and scrambled eggs. The day loomed ahead of me. In a town I had yet to navigate, every task felt like a great adventure. I had a batch of

"Live and work but do not forget to play. . . ."
—Eileen Caddy

mail to send off, but I had yet to find the post office. I knew, dimly, that it was in DeVargas Center, not far from Atrisco and green chili stew.

I slipped on slacks and a warm top, threw on my winter coat, and navigated the car out the slick driveway. I headed for DeVargas Center, mail in hand. Once in the mall, I asked directions to the post office. "The first left, by the jewelry store," I was told. I found the post office and found, to my relief, there was no line for service. I sent off a packet to my accountant and a packet of Christmas cards to the previous tenant. Sending off the mail gave me a feeling of accomplishment. Buoyed by a sense of success, I decided to try to find Cory's friend's silk shop. Why not take a conscious adventure? I piloted my little car toward Guadalupe. I took Guadalupe to Montezuma, parking on the street near a cluster of shops. I walked a block, looking for the silk shop. No luck. I was about to give up when I saw the sign for Sanbusco just ahead. Sure enough, when I opened the door to Sanbusco Market Center, I spotted a sign: SOULFUL SILKS, SINCE 1983. Cory's dog, Peaches, was sprawled at the entryway. I stepped past her into the shop, where Cory stood behind the counter.

"Boo," I said.

"You found it!" Cory exclaimed, coming out to give me a hug. All around us hung hand-dyed silk apparel: scarves, shawls, blouses.

"The palette keeps changing," explained Cory. "She keeps trying new things."

Cory herself wore soft cottons with a silken scarf looped around her neck. She was a good advertisement for the shop's wares.

"You can get a coffee or tea next door," Cory offered. "I just had a tea."

"Thanks." I pointed myself to the café next door. I ordered a raisin scone and a latte. I ferried my treats back to a table outside the silk shop. Cory joined me. The scone was too dry and the latte too weak. I fed crumbles of the scone to Peaches, who didn't find fault with her snack. A customer stepped into the silk shop and Cory excused herself to go help. From my table, I could watch through the shop window as the customer tried on scarf after scarf. Some were more flattering than others, and she finally settled on the very best. I watched her in pantomime as she protested the price. Cory stood firm. There was a twenty-five-percent-off sale in progress, but it was only for established customers on the shop's e-mail list.

"Try back tomorrow," Cory told the customer. "The owner will be in the shop then. I don't have the authority to change a price." Murmuring a somewhat resentful thank-you, the customer left the store. Cory rejoined me at the table.

"If you ever want to go to a movie, just give me a call," Cory told me. "I'm working several jobs, but I have a lot of freedom right now. Pretty soon I may open a café with a friend of mine. Then I won't have as much freedom."

"Sounds like an adventure!" I told Cory. "My meter's almost up. I'll let you go."

I reached my car with twelve minutes to spare. I piloted it around the corner on Montezuma and spotted an empty parking space in the lot for Borders. Entering the bookstore, I cast about for calendars.

"They're downstairs," a clerk told me.

Feeling disloyal to Tiger Lily, my dog, I chose a calendar featuring cats. Turning away from a calendar of New York, I selected one of the Grand Canyon instead. Both calendars were reduced in price to $4.99. I took them both and headed home with my loot. It had been a day of small adventures.

The prosperous heart thrives on adventure. New sights and sounds feed a feeling of abundance. Willing to focus time and energy in new directions, the prosperous heart remains authentic, true to itself in its likes and dislikes. Open to experimentation, it tries new

"The measure of mental health is the disposition to find good everywhere."
—RALPH WALDO EMERSON

ventures. An overflow of creative urges is the reward for indulging in the novel. The prosperous heart spills over into innovation.

WEEK FIVE CHECK-IN

Morning Pages: Did you do them this week? How many days?

Counting: Did you count this week? What did you learn?

Abstinence: Did you abstain from debting this week? If you did debt, what was it for? How did you feel?

Walking: Did you walk this week? What insights did you have?

Time-Out: Did you take your Time-Outs? What did you learn?

Prosperity Points

1. Assessing our inner circle is an important step in living our lives most fully, spending our time most prosperously.

Fill in the following sentences:

Today, my inner circle of people I see "live" includes:

1. _____

2. _____

3. _____

4. _____

5. _____

My inner circle of long-distance friends includes:

1. _____

2. _____

3. _____

4. _____

5. _____

I miss:

1. _____

2. _____

3. _____

4. _____

5. _____

I wonder if I should distance myself from:

1. _____

2. _____

3. _____

4. _____

5. _____

Look back over your lists. Are you inspired to call a long-lost friend? Are you inspired to hold your tongue a bit more with the nosy friend who calls every day?

2. Who in your inner circle offers a truly reciprocal relationship? Make a list of a few people you would enjoy having as guests in your home and invite them to a dinner party. If you are overwhelmed by the idea of cooking for everyone, ask each of your guests to bring a dish. Sharing recipes and culinary talents as well as conversation creates a deep sense of community, whether you are new to the community or not.

3. The prosperous heart is active on its own behalf. It does not languish, waiting for something to happen. Instead, it acts. There is *always* some small action we can take. The prosperous heart keeps moving forward. The prosperous heart believes in itself, and it believes, too, in a Higher Power. Taking time daily to check in with the Higher Power, the prosperous heart receives guidance. It knows which way to go, where and how to take a next step.

   Take an extra Time-Out and check in with yourself and your Higher Power. Ask what your next action regarding your finances should be. Are you surprised at what you "hear"? Our actions can be taken gently, with a prosperous heart. When we have a calm focus and a sense of clarity, we are ready to take action. We are changing, and the small steps we take will, in the long run, alter our trajectory significantly. We are becoming truly prosperous.

4. After taking a Time-Out, approach the following lists. Be gentle with yourself; these lists require you to dig deep into your financial and emotional past. Make your lists freely; act on them prudently. Making the lists and acting on the lists are separate tasks. For now, you are just exploring where action *may* be needed.

Fill in the following sentences:

In regard to my money, I resent:

1. _____

2. _____

3. _____

4. _____

5. _____

6. _____

7. _____

8. _____

9. _____

10. _____

Regarding money, I am jealous of:

1. _____

2. _____

3. _____

4. _____

5. _____

6. _____

7. _____

8. _____

9. _____

10. _____

In terms of my money, I feel codependently attached to:

1. _____

2. _____

3. _____

4. _____

5. _____

6. _____

7. _____

8. _____

9. _____

10. _____

Regarding my money, I regret:

1. _____

2. _____

3. _____

4. _____

5. _____

6. _____

7. _____

8. _____

9. _____

10. _____

In completing these lists, many people find it common for emotions to run high. Do not be alarmed. This is the beginning of integration, and an important part of recovery.

5. In looking back at your Counting, you have created a kind of "financial map": a detailed tracking of where your money goes. What do you see? What insight shocks you? Fill in the following sentences:

1. I need to say no to _____

2. I need to say no to _____

3. I need to say no to _____

4. I need to say no to _____

5. I need to say no to _____

6. I need to say no to _____

7. I need to say no to _____

8. I need to say no to _____

9. I need to say no to _____

10. I need to say no to _____

1. I need to say yes to _____

2. I need to say yes to _____

3. I need to say yes to _____

4. I need to say yes to _____

5. I need to say yes to _____

6. I need to say yes to _____

7. I need to say yes to _____

8. I need to say yes to _____

9. I need to say yes to _____

10. I need to say yes to _____

Be patient with yourself here. Making these lists does not mean you have to execute everything on them today. The actions you need to take can be done lightly, gradually.

6. Mentoring, and being mentored, fills us with hope. Fill in the following sentences:

    1. A great mentor in my life is _____

    2. A great mentor in my life is _____

    3. A great mentor in my life is _____

    4. A great mentor in my life is _____

    5. A great mentor in my life is _____

1. I could be a mentor to _____

2. I could be a mentor to _____

3. I could be a mentor to _____

4. I could be a mentor to _____

5. I could be a mentor to _____

1. I am inspired by _____

2. I am inspired by _____

3. I am inspired by _____

4. I am inspired by _____

5. I am inspired by _____

7. Open yourself to a new adventure. Stretch a little and step outside your comfort zone to experience something novel. It may be as simple as going to the movies by yourself.

   Fill in the following sentences:

   1. It would be fun to _____

   2. It would be fun to _____

   3. It would be fun to _____

   4. It would be fun to _____

   5. It would be fun to _____

6. It would be fun to _____

7. It would be fun to _____

8. It would be fun to _____

9. It would be fun to _____

10. It would be fun to _____

1. An adventure I'd like to take is _____

2. An adventure I'd like to take is _____

3. An adventure I'd like to take is _____

4. An adventure I'd like to take is _____

5. An adventure I'd like to take is _____

6. An adventure I'd like to take is _____

7. An adventure I'd like to take is _____

8. An adventure I'd like to take is _____

9. An adventure I'd like to take is _____

10. An adventure I'd like to take is _____

Choose an outing that feeds your heart. Give yourself at
least an hour of sheer play.

KINDNESS

This week you will be actively exploring the kindness of the universe, noting that there is indeed a "divine order" to our lives. This same kindness is yours to offer to yourself and to others. In return, you will receive the gifts of optimism and faith. You will begin to look for small tributes you can make to yourself. Treating yourself as a precious object makes you strong, and you are always rewarded for positive action on your own behalf. As you give to yourself, you have more to give to others. You will find that these gifts are appropriate, and often have nothing to do with money. And in giving to others in small loving ways, you are able to say yes to their gifts in return. In accepting the small gifts of life, you will open the door to the larger gifts, as well.

NEVER ALONE

At five thirty on a wintry Wednesday, there was a rap at my door. Tiger Lily barked a sharp "hello." I ushered in Brendalyn Batchelor, minister of the Unity Church of Santa Fe. She cradled a large box in her arms.

"Here it is," she said. "Your very own juicer."

"Wow. Set it on the kitchen table."

Brendalyn did as directed, stomping her feet, wet from the snow.

"I want to show you how this thing works," she said.

Brendalyn set about unpacking the juicer. She was a zealot, a juice devotee. I watched, apprehensive and fascinated.

"So now, this fits into this. You line up the red arrows. . . ."

Brendalyn has the pluck of a 1940s movie heroine. She is upbeat, feisty and very funny. As she put my juicer together with lightning speed, Tiger Lily hovered around her ankles. Brendalyn tried not to trip over her and gave a good-natured laugh.

"Tiger Lily has faith." Brendalyn smiled. "And she's hoping we have charity."

Brendalyn is a dog lover, herself the owner of a Labradoodle named Snickers. She was friendly toward Tiger Lily, but she was not to be deterred. The juicer was intricate to assemble and took a five-minute spiel to explain.

Brendalyn began chopping celery, cucumbers and apples. "You know what I think?" she said. "I think that when people are short on money, they feel like they can't give. So then they don't come to church, because they think we want their money, but really we just want *them*. They should come to church anyway."

"I think it's true, but I think it goes a little deeper," I replied. "When people are broke, they may be mad at God—or feel God is mad at them."

"Ooh, Julia. I think you're right. That's very insightful."

"And I think when people struggle to give, they also struggle to receive," I continued.

The juicer devoured the ingredients, spitting out juice.

"Try it," Brendalyn urged. I sipped the green juice tentatively. It was delicious.

"You can add cilantro or ginger," Brendalyn volunteered. "I like cilantro. And I think you're absolutely right. But I wish there were a way to tell everyone that God wants them to receive, no matter what."

"It just may not always be in the way we ask or expect."

"Yes," Brendalyn agreed. "It's amazing to me how our expectations can change how we feel. Yesterday I lost Snickers in the field behind the church for an hour. I thought I would die of fear. I was designing the 'lost dog' sign, trying to figure out how much I could afford as the reward, imagining crying myself to sleep—and then I thought, 'What am I doing?' I teach this stuff! I tried to imagine how happy I would be when Snickers was back in my arms. Five minutes later, he was."

"As if God were looking out for us after all," I said.

"Indeed," Brendalyn agreed, offering Tiger Lily a cucumber rind. Tiger Lily backed away, offended, as Brendalyn cackled with amusement. "Okay, Tiger Lily. I'll eat it myself."

I glanced at the clock. "Oops. It's nearly time for me to go pick up Rex and Michele. You can hold down the fort and play hostess."

"Who all is coming?" Brendalyn asked.

"Bill Maloney, Natalie Goldberg, Rick Bates and Baksim Goddard," I answered. I ducked out the door to the garage. As I backed my car into the snowy driveway, the four-wheel drive grabbed hold. A quarter mile drive down icy roads, I spotted Rex and Michele. They stood knee-deep in drifted snow, waiting at the end of their driveway for me.

I swung alongside and they clambered in, laughing.

"Thanks for doing this," Rex said.

"I had to. Tonight's lamb and pie. The whole menu is in honor of you."

Driving the slippery route back to my house, I found that even with four-wheel drive, the road was treacherous. We pulled into the driveway and slid into the garage. We picked our way into the house.

"It smells fantastic!" Rex exclaimed.

"You're carving," I told him. While he carved, I baked crescent rolls and made broccoli and pesto.

"Prosperity is not just having a lot of money. It is having a consciousness of the flow of substance."
—Eric Butterworth

"You carve like a professional," Brendalyn said to Rex.

The phone rang. Natalie and Baksim were lost. I gave them thorough directions and then went back to my other guests. Bill and Rick arrived just in time to help set the table. Bill's and Rick's conversation quickly became theological.

"I believe in prayer," Rick said. "I believe in letting God know what I am thinking."

"You make your God a father figure."

"No, I don't."

Bill is a Buddhist. Rick believes in a very personal God. Bill finds such a belief primitive.

This time I chimed in.

"You two can agree to disagree. All forms of faith are good," I said.

Natalie and Baksim were rapping at the door. I let them in, listening to their apologies.

"You're just in time," I told them. "Everything is ready. Help yourselves," I urged. "But first, a prayer from Brendalyn."

"May friendship nourish our souls as this meal nourishes our bodies. Amen," Brendalyn prayed. The guests fell to the food, heaping their plates high. We all retreated to the living room, where we found places on the comfortable leather couches.

"Lamb? Everything looks delicious," exclaimed Natalie. She and Baksim dug into their dinners. There was quiet for a while as everyone focused on their food. When several people went back for seconds, conversation resumed—theological again. "I've just read and am now rereading a book by Ernest Holmes called *This Thing Called You*. The first thirty pages are really impossible, but then the rest of the book is quite wonderful," I volunteered. I retreated to my bookshelves and came back with two spare copies. Rick was an eager taker. I had listened to Rick speak before and thought Holmes might be a good match for him.

"I don't believe God wants me to do a job I hate," he declared. "I'm praying for the next step. But I'm not my résumé, and I don't want to go back to what I did before."

"So you're waiting for God to find you a job?" Bill chimed in. "Yes."

"I think God helps those who help themselves. I think you've got to do something, not just depend on God."

"I am doing something. I'm praying."

"Something more like looking for a job."

"We'll see." Rick was obdurate.

Listening to Rick, I found myself thinking he had faith—reckless faith. I fully expected God to come through with help for him, but I thought it might be on God's terms, not Rick's. God might have business for him, and it might be doing a job he didn't like. Then again, maybe Rick was right, and God had something much better in store for him if he could just hold out. But holding out was standing awfully close to the abyss.

"Good luck to you then," someone said when Rick finished with his theory.

"Pie?" I asked. I carried the two pies to the living room coffee table. I went back to the kitchen and returned with vanilla ice cream. Brendalyn allowed that she was currently teaching a course on prosperity. "It's twelve weeks long and grounded in the twelve steps," she explained. She offered Rick a slot.

"I'd love to," he said. "But I'd have to juggle my schedule."

"Just know you're welcome," said Brendalyn. I wondered if she, too, felt he had a reckless faith. She was offering him a step back from the abyss. I offered him cherry pie, thinking he could use some comfort food. He was in such a precarious position.

Conversation now veered toward Buddhism. Natalie is a Zen Buddhist, and she easily joined in. Between bites of pie, she explained, "In Buddhism there is no God."

"When we commune with the spirit within and ask for new ideas, they are always forthcoming."
—Charles Fillmore

Put point-blank, her statement startled me.

"No God?" The idea seemed unthinkable. And, I thought, my comforting Ernest Holmes must seem childish to a Buddhist.

"Buddhists believe that we each possess the keys to our own enlightenment," Natalie said.

I looked out the window to the piñon trees. Tiny birds were still lighting on the feeders. Surely a god must have made them. A god must have made everything.

"Julia is a theist," Bill announced.

"I am," I concurred.

"What I can't stand are theist fundamentalists," he remarked.

"More pie?" I asked. I wondered whether I was a fundamentalist. Now I served up apple pie and ice cream.

"It's all divine," Rick announced.

"So, in Buddhism, is there no pie?" I joked, handing a slice to Bill.

"There's pie; it's just not this delicious." Natalie laughed.

The prosperous heart has humor, and so do my evening's guests. Their theological views are as varied as their thumbprints, and yet they peacefully coexist. The evening winds down on an amicable note. They agree on one thing, and that's the pie.

"Well, whatever gives us faith, I consider it a blessing." Brendalyn laughs, lightening the moment. "This pie gives me faith." The group laughs with her, connected again.

The prosperous heart is not lonesome. It has the companionship of God—or any Higher Power of our understanding—as well as of friends and colleagues. Rather than cling to lopsided loves, it basks in the company of kindred spirits. Guided by God, it chooses companions well. Not only are its own emotional needs met, it trusts that Spirit meets the needs of its beloveds. The prosperous heart affirms that there is more than enough to go around. God's storehouses are infinite. All are provided for if we ask. Our own prosperity does not diminish the prosperity of others.

KINDNESS TO SELF

Being kind to ourselves creates a prosperous heart. And yet being kind to ourselves can often take conscious effort. It is easy to be kind to others in need, but seeing our own needs clearly can take a little sleuthing.

I am teaching a workshop in Santa Fe now, and I ask the class how they could be kind to themselves. Protests arise.

"It is so much easier to be kind to my children than to myself," a woman in the front row says quietly, her eyes sad.

"Yes," I say. "And when you are kind to yourself, it is good for your children."

She lights up, hopeful. "Then it's not selfish?" she asks me, articulating the fear that we all encounter. We are afraid to be selfish. We are afraid that being kind to ourselves makes us selfish.

I ask the participants to break into clusters and discuss ways in which they could be kind to themselves. "Steal from one another," I tell them. "Observe ways that other people are able to be kind to themselves, and try the same."

The mother in the front row is now laughing in her cluster. I smile at her, wondering what she has uncovered. When we get back into the big group, she raises her hand.

"My cluster mate pointed out that children learn by example. If my children learn that I deprive myself for them, what am I teaching them?"

"That's true," I say. When I wrote *The Artist's Way,* my daughter, Domenica, was still a toddler. Underfoot, she learned to wait while

"Be a lamp, or a lifeboat, or a ladder. Help someone's soul heal."

—Rumi

"Mommy is writing." Now an adult, she is a writer herself. I have always loved—and kept—horses. Instead of putting that passion on hold when Domenica was young, I brought her into it. There is a photograph of me riding bareback with her as an infant in my arms. We are both laughing. Today, she has her own horse that she keeps at my sister Libby's ranch. I was able to share my passions with her rather than give them up on her behalf, and we both are richer for it.

Living in the West during parts of Domenica's childhood, I collected cowboy boots for both of us. New Mexicans wear their boots under skirts as well as blue jeans. The telltale pointy toe announces Western style. Whether worn in the kitchen or in the car, a cowboy boot announces freedom. "I'm doing what I choose to do," the boots say. Most owners flash at least two styles. There is the well-worn daily boot, and the carefully polished dress boot, worn only for special occasions. Brides wear them; grooms wear them; even the minister wears them.

Today, Domenica has a quick eye for a great pair of boots. A filmmaker by trade, she still dresses like a cowgirl. She wears a turquoise necklace, blue jeans, and boots. "Don't fuss with me," her apparel announces. "I'm not to be meddled with." And she is not.

"I like my boots because they are subtle," she says. She is referring to a black-and-cream pair of Old Gringo boots she wears most often. I watch her joy and am glad I indulged in cowboy boots for both of us—even though money was tight—when she was growing up.

Counting allows us to clearly see when we've indulged ourselves and when we've deprived ourselves. The outcome may surprise us.

"I realized that I'm totally happy to spend fifty dollars on dinner with a friend, but the twenty-dollar shampoo that would make me happy every day for months seems way too extravagant, out of the question."

"I happily spend outrageous amounts of money on designer shoes and jeans. But I refuse to buy myself nice underwear! What's that about?"

It is the small luxuries—the intimate ones only we know about or actually enjoy—that are usually the hardest to justify, but that add up to a life that feels truly luxurious. When we give ourselves small kindnesses, we open ourselves up to larger gifts, as well.

KINDNESS TO OTHERS

The prosperous heart is friendly. We no longer move through an adversarial world. Sourced in God, we see the divine spark in everyone we meet. We are not met by accident. We have spiritual "business" with one another. Sensing our lack of hostility, others meet us as kindred spirits. No longer competing, we meet as colleagues. There is enough good for all.

April has a prosperous heart. She knows the names of the diner's waiters. More than that, she knows their children's names. "How are they?" she always asks, and takes the time to listen. When April orders she says, "Please," and asks the waiter for what's good. Again, she listens carefully. Her courtesy makes her a favored customer. An outing to meet at the diner for a BLT is a chance to catch up on the neighborhood news. April's goodwill brightens everyone's day.

"Hi, Henry," she says to the beggar at the corner. "I see him every day. We might as well know each other's name," she explains.

Dogs as well as people meet with a cheery greeting. For my dog, April is a favorite, as she always takes the time to praise her beauty,

"There is but one cause of human failure. That is man's lack of faith in his true self."

—WILLIAM JAMES

noting when Tiger Lily has been for a "spa day" at the groomer. Although she leads a busy life, April spends her time and attention generously.

The prosperous heart derives sustenance from God's abundance. This makes it easy to be kind to others. As we are kind to others, we enable God to act through us. We become a channel for loving-kindness. Serving others with love, we serve our Creator. Sharing our kindness, in large and small ways, always brings us delight.

I glance out my window and see that my bird feeders aren't doing their usual business. I decide to take a break from writing and drive down to Wild Birds Unlimited. Once there, I find myself excited by the selection of seeds and feeders and the expertise of the staff. Santa Fe is a birding town—treating the migrators with kindness on their journey south. "My birds aren't finishing their seed cones," I tell the clerk.

"Crunch the final tidbits into a tray feeder," she suggests. I tell her my usual birds—juncos, nuthatches, chickadees, hairy woodpeckers, and flickers.

"You're doing well," says the clerk. "I'd stick with the same food, and maybe add some calcium. They need calcium right now, and they seek it out." She indicated a block of peanut butter–and–jelly suet. "This would be good," she says. I take two large cones of "supreme fair," although I wonder whether the larger-size cone might be too heavy for my feeders. "No," says the clerk. "They work quite well."

And so I pay my bill, forty dollars, and I accept the clerk's offer to lug my booty to the car. "It gets me out of doors," the clerk explains, and a cursory glance at her in baggy blue jeans and hiking shoes is enough to make it clear that she is, indeed, an outdoorswoman.

Back at home, I lug the heavy bag to my door, where Tiger Lily greets me with a pirouette of glee.

Treated with kindness in Santa Fe, I feel at home, safe, looked

"The Power which creates and sustains everything is now creating everything necessary to my happiness."
—Ernest Holmes

out for. As I look out for and treat my friends—human and avian—with kindness, I am rewarded by their appreciation and I am grateful to be of help to them. Small acts of kindness on our part can rescue another person's day.

The prosperous heart honors the special occasions of others: birthdays, anniversaries, events of all stripes. And it's not just about marking these occasions; it's being thoughtful toward other people in all ways—asking after sick relatives, acknowledging that someone has just started a new job, remembering—and using—people's names.

What small act of kindness could you take today?

LISTENING

When we listen to other people, we bear witness to their experience. We acknowledge them, their thoughts, their desires. So often all it takes to erase our worries is for someone to say, "I hear you." We can actively search out these people and these conversations.

When I was living in New York, I went through a trying medical situation that took several months to resolve. In the middle of my struggle, I was invited to a dinner party. That night I met an actress, Jennifer Bassey, whom I had previously known only in passing.

"I love your work," she said, sitting down next to me.

"And I love yours," I replied, pleased.

"We have so many friends in common," she noted, "but we don't really know each other. We should know each other. And you write plays. My husband wrote *Kismet*. He's delightful. You should be friends with him, too."

"In order to demonstrate prosperity, we must accept it mentally first."
—CATHERINE PONDER

Tickled by Jennifer's enthusiasm, I felt immediately comfortable with her. Her straightforwardness charmed me.

"So?" she asked. "What's going on?"

To my surprise, I found myself speaking candidly. After all, she was.

"Actually, I'm in kind of a fragile period. I have some medical issues that I'm working to straighten out."

Jennifer studied me closely, listening.

"Well, then," she said, "give me your phone number. I'll call you every day to see how you are. Once a day until everything is resolved."

Surprised but pleased, I handed her my number.

Jennifer was true to her word. She did call every day, offering her ear, her experience, her humor. By the time my health had stabilized, we were close friends. We still speak nearly every day. We check in just to check in—and to listen. In our friendship, no topic is off-limits. We listen to each other, and in listening, we cherish each other's daily experiences—and our own.

"Jennifer, it's snowing. I'm baking cookies and roasting a chicken for tonight's dinner. And I'm worried no one will make it here because of the weather."

"People will come. How much snow are you expecting?"

"I don't know. I think a lot."

"Well, you can always call and cancel. You can freeze everything and give people a rain check—or rather, a snow check."

Jennifer's good advice calmed me down. I took my two apple pies from the oven. I garnished a leg of lamb with garlic pepper, surrounded it with wild rice and mushrooms, and slipped the pan in to roast. My phone rang. It was Jennifer again, calling from New York.

"Darling. How are you doing now?"

"I've decided to go ahead with everything and let the chips fall where they may."

"You sound better."

"Yes, well, the snow seems to be letting up."

"Good, then, darling. I'll call and check on you later, but if you're midparty and you don't answer, I'll understand."

So often, what we crave is to be heard. So often, a two-minute phone conversation about "nothing"—i.e., exactly what is going on in that minute in our lives—means everything.

The prosperous heart listens. Do not underestimate how much this simple gift is worth. Whom can you call up today, "just" to listen?

SAYING YES

Saying yes is a way to be open to ourselves and others. It is a way to be open to the beauty of nature. It is a way to be open to life's small gifts—the fuchsia flower blooming in the window, the Jack Russell puppy who tears down the beach after his owner, the fancily hand-decorated cupcakes in the bakery display case. There are gifts for us at every turn—gifts of beauty, of humor, of love—if we are willing to accept them.

Santa Fe today is balmy. Although it is only mid-March, spring is afoot. Walking my dog, Tiger Lily, on the maze of dirt roads, I spot two robins. They dart across our path, en route to somewhere— perhaps even to my own bird feeders. There they will join the flocks of chickadees, nuthatches, and the occasional showy flicker. I have a special feeder just for blue jays, featuring unshelled peanuts. The robins may sample that, as well. It delights me that the birds accept my gifts.

"Trust in him at all times, O people; pour out your heart before him; God is a refuge for us."
—PSALM 62:8

Walking in the glorious weather, I find it easy to feel expansive. Although the winter was very beautiful, spring is more than welcome. Balanced on the cusp between the two, I find it easy to feel optimism. Back at home, I have turned off the gas stove in my writing room. There is enough warmth pouring through the windows. Walking along the road, I see the sun glinting off my neighbors' windows, warming their homes, too.

I have been in Santa Fe for six months now, and I feel I have barely scratched the surface of what this lovely city has to offer. My favorite luncheon spot is a restaurant called Counter Culture. The first item on its menu is something called a Fall Salad, featuring beets, gorgonzola cheese, and walnuts. Whenever I go to Counter Culture, I find myself ordering this salad. It is always delicious. But perhaps even more delicious is the large bulletin board on which a wide panoply of business cards have been tacked. There are cards for lawyers and cards for healers. There are cards touting crystals and cards inviting the reader to purchase hand-blown paper weights. All along one side of the board march invitations to explore the esoteric arts. There are psychics, mediums, and "intuitives." Packed just below these otherworldy invitations are several cards advertising good automobile mechanics. I like the pun in the name Counter Culture. Food is served over a counter, and the wide display of cards suggests a way of doing business that is indeed "counter" to the tried-and-true tradition of walking through the Yellow Pages.

Saying yes to Santa Fe, I find that much that seems exotic at first soon feels normal. Looking for a lawyer, I find one who owns two mustangs. We talk horses more than law over Starbucks coffees. I welcome and enjoy our common ground. In Santa Fe, inhabitants take the time to meet for breakfast, lunch, or dinner, valuing conversation and welcoming new relationships.

Meeting my fellow inhabitants, I discover that Santa Fe is a town full of readers. It's a pleasure to be told my books have been enjoyed—and not just *The Artist's Way,* either. Going to lunch, I find myself being treated to lunch. My fellow diners have a generous spirit, and I find myself enjoying their generosity.

Many people find being the recipient of goodwill gives them the feeling of being uncomfortably out of control. Accustomed to doing everything themselves and believing that they *must* do everything themselves, they turn away the help that is available to them. It is important to avoid the pattern of complete self-reliance, as it can ultimately be isolating.

Lana was right out of college when she was offered an internship at a powerful law firm. She hoped to go to law school and felt that the law firm would be the exact place she might work one day. Starting off strong, she was given—and accepted—great responsibility from her bosses. Seeing ways to improve systems they already had in place, she was proactive and generous with her help and ideas. But at the same time, Lana found herself slightly overwhelmed at her good fortune and the compliments she was receiving. She wondered whether she truly deserved the opportunity she was being given, and at her core, was afraid she did not.

Rather than trying to communicate her concerns with anyone, Lana started to retreat. In the evenings, rather than working on innovations for the company, she found herself watching TV and overeating to stuff her feelings of insecurity. As her weight climbed, her productivity dropped. Before long, she was slipping on her assigned duties, as well. Although she was well aware that her reputation with the company was declining, she felt somehow more familiar with the negative feelings than the positive attention she had been getting. Convinced that it was "too good to be true," and fraught with anxiety that her opportunity might somehow be taken away, Lana took the opportunity away from herself so she would feel that she was in control.

It is important to avoid the trap that Lana fell into. Feeling overwhelmed by positive attention or the generosity of others is common, but if we turn away from the goodwill that is offered to us, we risk turning against ourselves.

"The great promise of prosperity is that if men seek God and His righteousness first, then all shall be added unto them."
—CHARLES FILLMORE

The prosperous heart is not stingy. It relaxes into the moment at hand, recognizing that it is a gift both to give and to take. It allows others their generous impulses.

Back at home in my writing room, I glance out the window and laugh. The two robins are greedily helping themselves to the blue jays' peanuts.

WEEK SIX CHECK-IN

Morning Pages: Did you do them this week? How many days?

Counting: Did you count this week? What did you learn?

Abstinence: Did you abstain from debting this week? If you did debt, what was it for? How did you feel?

Walking: Did you walk this week? What insights did you have?

Time-Out: Did you take your Time-Outs? What did you learn?

Prosperity Points

1. Number from one to five. List five friends whose faith works for them.
   1. Michele. She is a devout Catholic and draws strength from the church.
   2. Sophia. She is active in AA, and the spirituality of the program shapes her life.
   3. Brian. He moved to the Unitarian Universalist church and seems much more at home there than where he was before.
   Etc.

2. Small acts of kindness toward ourselves pave the way to serenity, to a sense of optimism, and possibility.

Fill in the following sentences:

1. If it weren't too selfish, I'd _____

2. If it weren't too selfish, I'd _____

3. If it weren't too selfish, I'd _____

4. If it weren't too selfish, I'd _____

5. If it weren't too selfish, I'd _____

6. If it weren't too selfish, I'd _____

7. If it weren't too selfish, I'd _____

8. If it weren't too selfish, I'd _____

9. If it weren't too selfish, I'd _____

10. If it weren't too selfish, I'd _____

1. One way I could be kind to myself is _____

2. One way I could be kind to myself is _____

3. One way I could be kind to myself is _____

4. One way I could be kind to myself is _____

5. One way I could be kind to myself is _____

6. One way I could be kind to myself is _____

7. One way I could be kind to myself is _____

8. One way I could be kind to myself is _____

9. One way I could be kind to myself is _____

10. One way I could be kind to myself is _____

Answer the following question:
What could you adjust in your spending that would be an act of kindness to yourself?

1. I could ask the housekeeper to come every week instead of every other week.
2. I could buy a new needlepoint design and let myself take that up again.
3. I could buy my favorite fresh fruit and make fruit salads at home instead of buying the one in the cafeteria at work every day.
4. I could _____
5. I could _____

List ten luxuries under twenty dollars.
1. Fresh raspberries
2. A manicure
3. "Nicer" socks
4. A pound of great coffee
5. The new Alicia Keys album
6. A movie ticket
   Etc.
Now treat yourself to one.

3. Look at your calendar for the upcoming months. Note the special occasions of friends. Take yourself to a good

stationery store and purchase stationery or cards to send
out with personal greetings.

4. Name three people whom you see regularly but whose
    names you don't know. This week, find out—and use—
    their names.
    1. The evening waiter at the diner—Jimmy
    2. The good pharmacist—Mark
        Etc.

5. When was the last time you allowed someone to gift you
    with something? Take pen in hand and recall in detail
    your feelings of acceptance or resistance.

Week Seven

FORGIVENESS

At the midpoint of the course, it is important to acknowledge how far you have come. You have made great headway in clarifying your values, caring for yourself and your finances, and understanding who and what you desire to have in your life. You are ready now to let go of the past. In consciously letting go of feelings, beliefs, and circumstances that do not serve you, you open the door to allow the Higher Power to "copilot" your life.

It is time to forgive yourself, to forgive those who have wronged you (yes, *all* of them), and to move ahead in faith. If you have made mistakes with your finances, it is time to forgive yourself for those mistakes. If other people have wronged you, it is time to let go of resentment. In letting go of your negativity, you give yourself a gift. You will be amazed at the amount of energy forgiveness frees up, and you will be ready to move forward with enthusiasm.

FORGIVING OURSELVES

By this point in the course, Counting has become second nature. Our spending habits are becoming clear to us, and many of us have naturally adjusted our course in large and small ways. We have called our creditors and structured payment plans. As we send our first checks to repay our debts, we feel a sense of exhilaration. We know how much we owe. We know how much we have. We know that in our not debting, our numbers remain within our grasp. In practicing Abstinence, we become more comfortable. We feel a sense of relief as we finally begin to feel in control of our money, as opposed to having our money control us. We trust ourselves. Our money is just money. It is no longer a dark mystery, something we "could never understand." We have taken responsibility. We are beginning to know ourselves.

Yet part of us may recoil from this newfound knowledge. For what we discover are habits that may have been years in the making. As we bring our financial history into the light, we want to look away in embarrassment, in shame, in despair. On paper, out of the shadow of denial and in black and white, our mistakes blind us. How could we not have seen? We want to stop Counting. We want to shove our knowledge and our tools under the rug. We want a break from the painful clarity. We want to numb ourselves.

But we must not look away. Hiding is not the answer. There is a line in the Big Book of Alcoholics Anonymous that says, "Once an alcoholic has been exposed to AA, his drinking is changed forever." Our awareness of our money is also now changed forever. Our old habits work for us no longer. Like the dieter having an ice-cream binge in the middle of the night as an attempt to stave off loneliness, the reckless abandonment of our money tools does not give us the relief we seek. The morning after the ice-cream binge, we are bloated, sick, regretful. Ice cream did not take away our loneliness—in fact, it made it worse. We wash the spoon in the sink, scrub drops of melted ice cream off the counter, and wonder who did this to us. Abandoning our money tools is the same. A midnight online shopping spree does nothing to ward off our fears. The next morning, the confirmation e-mails sit in our in-box. Purchases we don't need are on their way. We look at our account balance and wonder who did this to us.

For the mistakes we have made and the mistakes we will make,

"What we are today comes from our thoughts of yesterday, and our present thoughts build our life of tomorrow."
—THE BUDDHA

we must forgive ourselves. Loneliness is what we feel when we push God out of our lives. Forgiving ourselves invites a Higher Power into our lives, easing our sense of isolation. In forgiving ourselves, we allow God to help us. In allowing God to help us, we open the door for true prosperity to enter our lives.

Paula, a young mother in my class, stubbornly stays in an unhappy marriage because her lawyer husband makes a lot of money and stands to inherit even more. "I have twins," Paula wails. "I can't afford to raise them alone. It's easier to deal with my husband's mood swings than to try to live without his money."

But is it? Is Paula's lifestyle worth the price she pays for it? Do her children really benefit from the choice she is making for them? Paula's materialism looms large. She must forgive herself for her dependence, and place her faith squarely with the Higher Power.

I ask my students to write about situations or events that they need to forgive themselves for. "Fill in the following sentence," I say. "'I need to forgive myself for . . .'"

John, another student in my class, is deeply angry as he recalls an act of self-sabotage from his past. "I can't forgive myself," he says darkly. "I wrote a screenplay in my twenties that was optioned by a studio. I spent the option money and I never delivered the rewrites. The option ran out. Now I see that I procrastinated. To me, that's unforgivable. I feel like I was lazy and careless, and I can never get that opportunity back." John clenches his fists in his lap.

From the front of the room, I feel excited for John. His denial is breaking. "Procrastination is not laziness," I tell him. "It is fear. Call it by its right name, and forgive yourself."

John raises his hand. His demeanor is softening as he writes, and I am interested to hear what he is thinking. "I feel completely crazy," he says, "but I just got an idea. I probably can't go back to the studio where I never delivered the screenplay, but I *can* write another

"Change, even when it's for the good, can be frightening. But if you are going to transform your life through a journey to prosperity, you must try to learn to welcome change."
—Edwene Gaines

screenplay. I have a notebook full of ideas. If I write because I want to write, because I love movies, I bet I'll have fun."

"I bet you will," I say to John. And I wouldn't be surprised if John sells another screenplay down the road, either.

When we forgive ourselves, we make way for hope, for optimism. When we forgive ourselves, we make way for God to help us. At first, it may feel awkward asking God to take over our affairs. It is somehow so intimate. And yet God knows all the details of our lives, and pretending that he doesn't gets us nowhere. Better to admit to the intimacy that exists already. Better to further that intimacy. "You handle it, God," we can say, and that lessens our worry. "God's got it," we remind ourselves. But this does not let us off the hook of responsibility. We still have to act on our own behalf. We can also, though, ask for help and guidance. We are never alone. In dire times, God is not paralyzed as we might be. No circumstance is beyond God's healing powers. The prosperous heart asks for help, confident that help will come. Asking, it believes it will receive. Asking for forgiveness, we forgive ourselves.

"I expect everything I do to prosper. I enthusiastically expect success."

—Ernest Holmes

FORGIVING OTHERS

There are few emotions as uncomfortable as resentment. An old saying sums it up well: "We drink the poison and then wait for the other person to die." Resenting others, we do poison ourselves. When our energy is spent on imaginary fights with those who have wronged us, we are not present in our day-to-day life. We have poisoned our own well.

"But, Julia!" my student protests. "You don't understand. My ex-wife has truly wronged me. Every day, she makes my life a living hell. I think she's made it her life's purpose to torture me."

There are *always* those one or two people who we are so sure are in the wrong. And they may well be—but so are we, as long as we are stewing in resentment toward them, going back over what they have done, or jumping into the future, fantasizing about what they *might* do. As long as those people are living rent-free in our minds, we are not free to prosper.

When we are stuck in this destructive cycle, the person who is most hurt is *us*. We aren't just suffering in the moment of attack; we are reliving that moment over and over. We rehearse what we should have said, what we will say next time. We create stories about what our next interaction with these people will be—how they will hurt us, how we will hurt them. We are caught in an obsession.

So what do we do? Mired in our woes, we are stuck. Like the person caught in an avalanche, not knowing which way is up, we feel out of control, smothered, as if we will never see the light again.

The answer is very simple. Pray for the person you resent.

"What?" my students always exclaim. "I can't do that. Anything but that. *Pray* for them? I don't even know how to pray!"

"Wish them well," I say. "Pray that they get everything *you* want for yourself."

Mayhem. The class is revolting, protesting. People are looking at one another desperately, glaring at me, slamming notebooks shut.

"Try it," I say calmly. "What happens if you try it?"

A girl in the front row raises her hand. "I was sexually abused by my uncle. I *cannot* pray for him. I want to kill him."

"Do you see how these emotions are hurting you?" I ask her gently.

"Yes," she says, her eyes filling with tears. "He's making me crazy, and he doesn't even know I am thinking of him."

"Right," I say. "What is your uncle's name?"

"Carl."

"Whatever you ask in prayer, believe that you have received it, and it will be yours."

—MARK 11:24

"I'd like you to write the following phrase down ten times: 'God bless Carl.' See what happens."

She begins to write. Her courage inspires those around her. Other students take deep breaths, open their notebooks, uncap their pens. I wait.

"Take a deep breath," I say when they are finished. "What was your experience with that exercise?"

After a moment, the girl in the front row raises her hand. "I can't believe it," she says, her eyes wide. "At first, it felt terrible to write the words 'God bless Carl.' I thought that by praying for him, I was saying that what he had done was okay. But I started to have thoughts I've never had before. At first, I thought I just hated him. Then it dawned on me that he's very sick, and that has nothing to do with me. So many therapists have told me that, but I never 'got it' myself until it occurred to me right now. Then the more I wrote, 'God bless him,' the more I realized that maybe I meant, 'God *take* him.' He's not my problem. He's God's problem."

Indeed. Those who have hurt us are God's problem—and God can handle them. It is not God's will for us to stew in resentment, missing out on our lives.

Always, one hundred percent of the time, when we are stuck in resentment, we are avoiding ourselves. There is always a productive action lurking nearby, waiting patiently for us to take it. Focused on how the line producer has wronged us with his snarky attitude, we are not focused on the script rewrites we need to deliver. Focused on our neighbor's nosy gossip, we are not focused on the flowers waiting to be planted on our side of the fence. Planting the flowers on our side of the fence will heal us—and put our neighbor in perspective.

Oscar Wilde once said, "Always forgive your enemies; nothing annoys them so much." Taking our attention off those who have wronged us and putting it onto ourselves, we reclaim our power. When we are focused on the beauty of our own flower garden, the nosy neighbor has little to dig her claws into. When we nurture ourselves, there is less room for negativity in our psyche, and we have less negativity in our lives.

The prosperous heart admits to all of its feelings. Rather than deny or lash out when "bad" feelings occur, the prosperous heart accepts the full range of human emotion. Acceptance holds the key to freedom. If we can admit how we feel, our emotions become fluid and able to change. Praying for those who have wronged us is a positive use of the energy we are *already* spending on the people we wish we weren't thinking of at all. Instead of driving ourselves crazy with resentment, through forgiveness we free ourselves of their destructive power over us. If we can pray for those who have hurt us, we will have taken the first steps toward forgiveness of others, and the first steps toward living our lives most fully.

DISMANTLING NEGATIVITY

Negativity is always a front for fear, and compassion will always dismantle it. In improv comedy, there is a technique called "agreeing and contributing." One actor cannot negate what the other has just said, or the improv will slow to a stop. The response must be, "Yes and . . ." to keep the scene moving. Our lives are the same: it's up to us whether we respond positively or negatively to others, whether we assume there is something we can learn from or build on in our relationships, or we tear them down, brick by brick.

My landlady has phoned, wondering whether I will be renewing my lease and staying in the little house for another year. "Yes," I tell her. Although many of my friends have fancier homes, I have come to love the snug little adobe I have chosen.

"For those who believe, no proof is necessary. For those who don't believe, no proof is possible."
—John and Lyn St Clair-Thomas

"Be alert for bears," warns Julie, who used to live in my neighborhood. The idea of bears seems far-fetched, but, Julie warns, two people were killed by bears last year. "You really should take your bird feeders inside every night."

"Really?" I say, knowing that I will not follow her suggestion. My porch lights cast a circle of illumination in which a bear would be spotted. "I worry more about snakes than bears," I tell her. "But up here in the piñons, rattlesnakes are scarce."

"Bull snakes are common, though," she says, stubbornly negative. Any snake at all is one too many from my perspective. I get off the phone and shudder.

Tonight is Wednesday, my night for company. But another phone call informs me that two of the invited guests are feuding, not a problem I'm accustomed to. "Just keep your eyes open," warns the caller. I wonder exactly what damage could be done. I don't like the implied threat, and I do like the guest who the caller claims is the instigator.

Santa Fe is a small city. People know one another, and gossip seems particularly malevolent. I find myself wanting to place principles before personalities. I don't care to choose sides with my guests. I want to believe in the essential goodness of all the people I've invited. Being wary of my guests strikes me as paranoia, not unlike the warning about bears. Yes, something bad *could* happen, but the odds seem against it. Just for tonight, I'm going to try to assume all is well.

Two negative phone calls in a row, and I am wondering what is in the air. When negativity seems to come to us from out of left field, it is easy to feel shaken, to take it personally. But negativity always comes from fear—fear of not getting what we want, fear of losing what we have, fear of being judged, fear of being ignored. When other people spew their negativity onto us, we can look for the fear that is lurking underneath. We will always find it.

"Life is a mirror and will reflect back to the thinker what he thinks into it."
—Ernest Holmes

Last week, when I taught a workshop, the host approached me before I stepped onstage.

"I find with our audiences, you have to get their attention right away. Otherwise, they'll figure you don't know what you're talking about and they won't come back."

Taken aback, I tried not to break my focus as I prepared to speak. His "words of wisdom" were not helpful. But looking back now, I see he was speaking out of fear. He was in his first year directing the center—a center that is in financial trouble. The first six months of his tenure had had mixed results. The first program he'd hosted was well reviewed, but a financial disaster. The next two were smaller, steady, but not the "slam dunk" he was looking for. He was hoping I would be his star speaker, the one who would make him look good. Desperation in his eyes, he acted defensively. But he was afraid. Afraid of losing his job, afraid of looking bad, afraid of not being a star. Approaching his work from the outside in, he will stay afraid. Approaching his work from the outside in, he is unlikely to be authentically successful. "God bless you," I think, recalling his face. I will not return to teach there again.

Other people's negativity is best avoided as much as possible. Whenever possible, we must keep close to those whose optimism matches our own. But likewise, we must look at ourselves. When we are afraid, do we carelessly spew negativity out into the world? Do we consider how we affect others in these moments?

I have one day left before I must fly back to New York to teach. As always, I am nervous about the flights. I once told my psychiatrist about my fear of flying. He listened gravely, and then said, "Yes. When you agree to fly, you agree to the possibility that you might be a fatality."

"Yikes," I thought. "For this I'm paying a hundred and eighty dollars an hour?" His advice did little to soothe me.

Next I phone the woman who is driving me to the airport.

"Your prosperity consciousness is not dependent on money; your flow of money is dependent on your prosperity consciousness."
—Louise Hay

"How are you?" she asks.

"I'm nervous," I tell her. "I'm always nervous about flying."

"Yes," she says, "it's too bad you can't just do a couple of shots." She well knows that a couple of shots are out of the question for me. She also does little to soothe me. My next call is to New York, to the Open Center, where I will be teaching.

"Sandy," I ask the director, "is everything prepared?"

"Yes," she assures me. "How are you?"

"Anxious," I reply, not explaining, and not thinking about whether this answer might make *her* anxious.

Now I call my friend Rex, who also picks up on the nervousness in my voice.

"You're going to be fine," he says firmly. "Everything will go well. What have you been up to this morning?"

His question startles me, and I laugh, realizing suddenly that I have spent the morning complaining about my nerves to everyone who will listen.

"I guess I've been worrying. And talking about it . . . to everyone."

Rex laughs kindly. "I've been there," he reassures me. "You're just scared."

His honest—and accurate—assessment puts me immediately at ease.

"I need to get off the phone now," I tell him. "I owe Sandy a reassuring call."

Rex chuckles. "I've been there, too. She'll appreciate the call," he says. "And, Julia—don't beat yourself up. Everyone worries about stuff."

When I let myself peer beyond the edges of my anxiety, I find I am excited at the chance to teach. I have taught at the Open Center for seventeen years, and I love my New York students. They are both gritty and grateful. They have a good sense of humor and enough energy to pilot their way through a long day of teaching. I

"So then, whenever we have opportunity, let us work for the good of all."
—Galatians 6:10

have spoken with Emma, who tells me that both she and Tyler will be on tap for my teacher's day. I am grateful for their help. I know that just having them present will guarantee that I stay steady and teaching at the top of my form. Grateful to be feeling grateful, I realize that I will treat everyone with more grace as I keep my own fears in perspective.

The prosperous heart feels secure and does not go looking for trouble. The prosperous heart knows that negativity is born from fear.

When has someone else's negativity shaken you? Looking below the surface, do you see their fear?

What are you feeling negatively about? What fear is lurking behind this feeling?

MOVING FORWARD

When we take risks, we experience the feeling of being in love with ourselves. If for this reason alone, risks are worth taking.

Jim was out of work. After eighteen years of steady, well-paid employment, he lost his job when his company downsized. He mailed out over a hundred résumés, but the response was scanty. Rather than panic, Jim used his time out of work to reflect. He realized that no job would make him happy, because the city he lived in no longer seemed to meet his needs.

"I realized I didn't like it here," Jim says. "This city is concrete and glass. I miss nature." Jim's ego had kept him in the big city. His heart yearned for a more human scale.

Jim decided to listen carefully to his discontent. He realized he was no longer enthralled by the city's frantic pace. As a younger man, he had found the hustle and bustle invigorating. The city's ambition matched his own. Now he found his values had shifted.

"You can cleanse your mind for prosperity by getting things in order generally."
—CATHERINE PONDER

What mattered to him now was love. This fact astonished him, but it was true.

"It sounds corny, but I craved family," Jim says. "I had put family at a distance twenty years before. My family lived on the West Coast and I elected to move east. For two decades I was the lone wolf, and my family ties languished. Now I found myself craving connection."

Jim reached out to his family, and, to his delight, they reached back to him. The renewed contact felt wonderful, and Jim found himself yearning to be closer than a long-distance call. Further soul-searching led him to a startling decision: he would move back west, looking for an apartment and a job near his family. Once the decision was made, the move transpired smoothly. He was welcomed back into the family fold like a prodigal son.

"I'm so grateful that I found the courage to move," Jim says. "It was novel for me, listening to my heart." Jim went from having an anxious, ego-driven life to having a prosperous heart. He resolved to listen to his heart and make decisions reflecting his true values. This meant he now sought meaningful work and not just a high paycheck. This change was nothing short of a revolution.

Allowing ourselves to see our options, no matter what the situation, is an invaluable doorway to freedom. It takes courage to step out of our comfort zone and open ourselves to the opportunities available to us, but as we accept even the smallest steps as progress, we are rewarded with self-confidence.

Rodrigo is a young, ambitious man whose gifts as a communicator and performer are obvious to anyone who knows him. Nurtured in high school by a speech and drama teacher who saw and pushed his talents, Rodrigo was used to putting many hours a day into working on a speech, rehearsing for a play, studying a script, writing a song. Accustomed to using his creativity constantly, he felt untethered whenever a project ended.

Rodrigo was between high school and college when he accepted

"I know that I am drawing my good to me. There is a silent power of attraction within me which is irresistible."
—Ernest Holmes

a summer office job to earn money for school. Although it was for only three months, within the first week he found himself discouraged by sorting papers. "This isn't who I am," he thought to himself as he transferred files from one person's desk to another. Frustrated by the sense that his creativity was stifled in the office environment, he was tempted to quit the job. But quitting wasn't an option; he needed the money. Even though he reminded himself that it was "only" three months, he wondered how he would survive the summer.

Rodrigo was determined to not be discouraged, though. He remembered a comedy class he had taken in high school. There had been an assignment to take a "plain"-looking experience and find the humor in every corner of the situation. Suddenly, he knew what he would do with his summer job. He would write a one-man show. It would be a comedy set in an office, from the perspective of the intern. He began to go to work looking forward to the anecdotes he would find in his day. The nasty mail lady who had annoyed him was now a rich character. He could hardly wait to see what she would say when she delivered the mail to his boss. Filled with energy and purpose, he came home and wrote at night. By the end of the summer he had written his show. When he got to college, he performed an excerpt of it at an open mike. The response was fantastic, and a student producer offered to produce the show at a coffeehouse on campus. From there, it transferred to a small theater.

Today, Rodrigo has written and performed many of his own works. His one-man show has been performed by himself and others. He is also a teacher, and his students are always thrilled by the idea that his first show was based on a "sort of" true story, but more thrilled by what it suggests: that we are able to find inspiration and creative motivation *anywhere* we are determined to look for it. We always have the opportunity to move ahead.

"God doesn't have what you need. God is what you need."
—Eric Butterworth

The prosperous heart is daring. It trusts its own impulses and is not afraid to strike out in new directions.

WEEK SEVEN CHECK-IN

Morning Pages: Did you do them this week? How many days?

Counting: Did you count this week? What did you learn?

Abstinence: Did you abstain from debting this week? If you did debt, what was it for? How did you feel?

Walking: Did you walk this week? What insights did you have?

Time-Out: Did you take your Time-Outs? What did you learn?

Prosperity Points

1. Forgiveness paves the way to self-acceptance and freedom. Hint: you need to forgive yourself for anything that triggers feelings of self-loathing, of fear, of resentment. Any highly charged negative emotion is fertile ground for forgiveness. Fill in the following sentences:

    1. I need to forgive myself for paying Thomas six months ahead "in good faith." I was wrong about trusting Thomas.

    2. I need to forgive myself for having credit-card debt.

    3. I need to forgive myself for putting my painting career on hold.

    4. I need to forgive myself for _____

    5. I need to forgive myself for _____

6. I need to forgive myself for _____

7. I need to forgive myself for _____

8. I need to forgive myself for _____

9. I need to forgive myself for _____

10. I need to forgive myself for _____

Now, "acting as if" we *already* forgive ourselves, fill in the following list:

1. I completely forgive myself for paying Thomas.
2. I completely forgive myself for staying in my marriage too long.
3. I completely forgive myself for letting my option run out.
4. I completely forgive myself for _____

5. I completely forgive myself for _____

6. I completely forgive myself for _____

7. I completely forgive myself for _____

8. I completely forgive myself for _____

9. I completely forgive myself for _____

10. I completely forgive myself for _____

Number from one to five. List five arenas, great to small, in which you could use God's help to forgive yourself.

1. My diet. I really want to lose weight.
2. My bedroom. I need to keep it neater.

3. The financial state of my business. I want to keep it
   running.
   Etc.

2. Admitting where we feel resentment is the first step to
   letting go of it. Don't judge yourself or assume you are
   being petty. As fast as you can, so that you don't overthink
   this, fill in the following sentences:

   1. I resent _____

   2. I resent _____

   3. I resent _____

   4. I resent _____

   5. I resent _____

   6. I resent _____

   7. I resent _____

   8. I resent _____

   9. I resent _____

   10. I resent _____

   Try this simple exercise with the same person you resent
   most:

   1. God bless _____

   2. God bless _____

   3. God bless _____

4. God bless _____

5. God bless _____

6. God bless _____

7. God bless _____

8. God bless _____

9. God bless _____

10. God bless _____

Notice your emotions. By the tenth time you fill in the person's name, what are you feeling? What new thoughts are occurring to you?

Now, take pen in hand and write about one negative interaction with another person. Ask God to bless the other person. Can you feel a shift occurring as acceptance replaces resentment? Can you see that this person is God's problem, not yours? What positive action have you been avoiding while this person has remained unforgivable?

3. Moving forward in small, authentic ways puts us in touch with inspiration.

Fill in the following sentence twenty-five times:

1. I wish _____

2. I wish _____

3. I wish _____

4. I wish _____

5. I wish _____

6. I wish _____

7. I wish _____

8. I wish _____

9. I wish _____

10. I wish _____

11. I wish _____

12. I wish _____

13. I wish _____

14. I wish . . . _____
    Etc.

The wish list is a powerful tool. Seemingly sweet and harmless, it is actually very potent. It dismantles our denial, and can leave us feeling exposed and vulnerable. For this reason, the exercise should be done quickly. Velocity leads to veracity. We tell the truth on the page. That truth may surprise and humble us. We are often surprised by what we wish for. And yet those wishes may have the power to change our lives.

Week Eight

VELOCITY

This week you will be creating another inventory, but instead of being focused on money, it is focused on *time*. At this point in the course you may find yourself anxious about time: you feel you have too much; you feel you don't have enough; you feel you've wasted time; you feel impatient. The truth is that you do have enough time and you are right on schedule, but it will take a little self-reflection to believe this. The good news is that you have energy. This week you will uncover the ways this energy is best focused.

Too much velocity upsets the apple cart, but too little velocity causes us to feel stagnant. This week is about finding the balance. The proper amount of velocity is something you find through doing your Morning Pages and your Counting.

SLOWING DOWN

In a culture of cell phones and iPads, where our job is in our pocket, we are constantly bombarded by requests for our time and attention. As the velocity of our lives increases, it becomes even more important that we do Morning Pages and take Time-Outs. Tempting as it is to check our devices each time they make a sound, the constant distraction is actually a route to less—not more—productivity.

Too many demands on our consciousness create a sort of mental logjam. Demands frequently contradict one another, and all of them claim our attention. The hustle and bustle of modern life can leave us paralyzed, unable to act effectively on our own behalf. The solution is not to speed up, but rather, to slow down. Taking the time for Morning Pages and Time-Outs allows us to slow down and get in touch with the deeper currents of ourselves. We learn how we really feel, and why. Without the excessive blur of high velocity, we are free to be our authentic selves.

It's a Friday morning. My phone rings and it is Michele, calling to invite me out to dinner. She and her husband, Rex, want to repay me for the many Wednesday nights they have come to my house. It isn't necessary, but it's nice.

"That would be lovely," I reply. We agree to rendezvous at a restaurant called Zia. The menu features comfort food.

"I'll have meat loaf," I say. Rex and Michele request burgers. Our waitress is pert and solicitous. She fusses over our orders.

Rex and Michele moved to Santa Fe from Los Angeles, where they both had enjoyed booming careers. Rex is a writer and painter. Michele is a fashion stylist. Although grateful for the lifestyle they can now afford in their retirement, they find themselves at loose ends since moving to Santa Fe. There is not the busy push they were accustomed to. Without the excitement of a high-speed existence, they find themselves having to dig deep, asking themselves, "Who am I without my brilliant career?" I am asking myself the same question. At times, I catch myself wondering whether I am too ambitious for Santa Fe. My life in New York was stressful and demanding. I wrote book after book; I attended theater and concerts; I taught and traveled. In New York, I had an identity. I was a working writer, with the emphasis on *working*. In Santa Fe, my writing hours are shorter and I spend more evenings at home. Like Rex and Michele, I must redefine myself.

There has to be more to life than work, I tell myself. I have my

"Prayer is an attitude of the heart."
—Larry Dossey

Wednesday night soirees. I have my weekly Artist Dates. Daily, I have the unaccustomed quiet of my house. There are no horns or sirens. There is, instead, the unexpected sighting of a northern flicker working away at the bird feeder, a large, striking bird that chases the smaller birds away. Maybe my life will boil down to birding, I tell myself.

The anxious heart is a hurried heart. Always wanting more, it grabs at experience like a greedy child, never satisfied. The prosperous heart, by contrast, matches its pace to God's. There is no rush. There is no hurried apprehension. Praying for knowledge of God's will, it sees that will in the pacing of its blessings. Savoring every moment, it feels a sense of abundance. The prosperous heart enjoys the luxury of time. There is enough time, it affirms. There is always time enough. Each moment comes as quickly as it should—or as slowly. Life attains a sense of spaciousness. There is a calm in its unfolding. Slowing down, taking things one at a time, we may still find life moving at a rapid pace. God can move very quickly but without the frantic sense of pell-mell the anxious heart is accustomed to. As we relax into God's timing, we find ourselves carried along as if on a wave in the ocean. Life unfolds without our hurried effort. We ask daily for our marching orders and receive an intuition of our priorities for the day. God's pace may at first feel dangerously slow. We are accustomed to pushing forward; now we're being asked to relax. This may give us a feeling of vertigo, a sense of falling through wide swaths of unstructured time and space. But when we relax, we realize that we are not in free fall, but are fully and gently supported by our Higher Power.

In New York, I would rush from event to event. My friends, like myself, were busy—too busy to see one another, it sometimes seemed. The phrase "I'm working" had a certain unassailable righteousness about it. Our brilliant careers were the focus of our lives. "I can see

"And the Lord will make you abound in prosperity."
—Deuteronomy 28:11

you in March," a busy friend told me in January. Instead of protesting, I meekly agreed. March would be fine and here soon enough.

In Santa Fe, I find myself insisting on a different life. I cook for my new friends every Wednesday. I make time for coffee dates. I phone my friends just to say hello. I will not wait for March to roll around in order to get together. To put it succinctly, I am slowing down. I am curbing my velocity. I want to experience a sense of prosperity that can be experienced only when life has some leisure in it. "Easy does it" is my new motto. I still show up at the page to write, but my quota of pages is smaller. And I allow phone calls to interrupt me.

My friend Sophia found that slowing down actually felt perilous. A workaholic long accustomed to pushing herself forward, she found that giving up velocity frightened her. Yet she resolved to slow down.

"I began to pray for God's will for me instead of just assuming that God's will for me was work and more work," she says. "I began to take life one day at a time and discovered that each day contained enough forward motion. Without pushing, I found myself actually accomplishing more. I prayed to be a conduit, and God took me up on my prayer."

Sophia had an anxious heart, but she soon found that by slowing down her headlong pace, her heart grew more prosperous. Slowing down, she was able to sense God as a constant companion. "I found myself feeling connected to a benevolent Something," she recalls. "I used to pray and rush forward, never pausing to hear a response. Now I pray and feel the answer forming. I wait quietly for the still, small voice to speak to me—and it does."

Indira Gandhi stated the case succinctly: "You must learn to be still in the midst of activity and to be vibrantly alive in repose."

When we are "alive in repose," we are receptive. We are able to

"It is your birthright to be prosperous, regardless of who you are or where you may be."
—Charles Fillmore

receive the good the universe has to offer us. Too often, the anxious heart is closed.

"In the middle of difficulty lies opportunity," Einstein observed, but the anxious heart is often blind to opportunity. Racing ahead too fast, it feels buffeted by difficulties, not seeing the silver linings. The prosperous heart, by contrast, sees the good contained in apparent hardship. Taking the time to look, it finds its attention rewarded.

"MAYBE TOMORROW . . ."

We are made anxious by a life filled with too much velocity. But a life with too little velocity also hinders us. "If I only had more time, I'd make my art," we say. Or, "If I only had more money, I could afford to take the time to paint. . . ." But this is untrue. Great swaths of time before us can be intimidating. Relieved of any excuse, we feel pressured to perform. Instead, we are often most productive when we have limited time. Why do we produce our catchiest tune when we have only half an hour to write the song? Why do our best ideas come to us in the shower, while we are merging on the freeway, when we're on the subway, moving from one appointment to the next?

Sometimes the flow of images triggers our creativity. Sight leads to insight. If we make the pace of our lives too slow, we risk becoming stagnant.

My neighbor Annette is a costume designer. Once sought after on Broadway, she let her work take a backseat to the demands of her husband's job. A corporate mogul, he moved often as his success grew, and Annette moved with him. Leaving New York, she left Broadway behind her. Unavailable to work, she was replaced by other designers.

Her husband's work proved very lucrative, and she lent her artistic eye to the design of every new house they moved into, each one more beautiful and lavish than the last. In each new city, she promised herself she would get involved in the local theater. She could donate her talents; she could teach; she could mentor. In each new house, she hired an organizer to help create the perfect room for her many bolts of beautiful fabric, for her trays of buttons and zippers, beads and ribbons. But she never entered the rooms. She never involved herself in the community. Setting up eight new sewing rooms—rooms that would rival most costume shops—in fifteen years, she never sewed anything.

"I feel so guilty," she told me over tea in my kitchen. "I really have the perfect setup. And I don't use it. It's like having a huge playroom but not letting the children in. I can't understand what is wrong with me."

"You need to coax yourself. Try making something tiny," I told her. Clearly, Annette didn't do anything tiny. Dripping with jewels and dressed in highly dramatic outfits, Annette had pipe dreams of elaborate costumes.

"Something tiny? That never occurred to me," Annette exclaimed. "Let's see . . ." She cast about my kitchen, thinking, as Tiger Lily trotted in, looking for food.

"Tiger Lily!" Annette caroled. "You're my inspiration! Look at that black collar. We can do better, can't we?" Tiger Lily continued sniffing around her food bowl.

"How about that?" Annette laughed. "I'll make Tiger Lily a crazy collar."

"That's a good start," I told her. The next day, Annette arrived with four collars. Velvet, silk, and leather, they were beautiful.

"One for each season," she said. "Tiger Lily needs to keep up with the trends."

Annette was visibly brightened by her small project. Her eyes

"You are the light of the world. Go forth and shine brightly."
—EDWENE GAINES

shone with pride as she placed the first collar around Tiger Lily's neck. "There you go, beauty," she crooned.

It is a common assumption that all the time and money in the world will make us happy people, will make us productive artists, will bring us contentment. But all the time in the world is daunting. And while all the money in the world will keep a roof securely over our heads, it will not feed our soul. It is up to us to feed our souls. Making art, expressing ourselves in small ways, these are the things that bring us to a prosperous heart. The danger of living a life in which everything is "taken care of" is that we get much too comfortable. And getting too comfortable can be very uncomfortable.

It is satisfying to be active. Taking ourselves out of our comfort zone in small ways can lead to a sense of purpose and hope.

"Whatever the conscious mind thinks and believes, the subconscious identically creates."
—BRIAN ADAMS

OBSESSION

Wherever there is ambiguity or uncertainty, there is room for obsession. When we are uncertain about our finances, it is easy to obsess over the things we can't control—what the stock market will do tomorrow or next year, whether our competitor's business will succeed or fail, what our accountant will be able to pull off with our taxes. When we are caught in an obsession, we cannot find clarity. It is quite possible that we enter an obsession to *avoid* clarity.

Obsession is a debilitating loop, a dark trail we follow deeper and deeper into the wrong woods. "Does he love me?" we ask ourselves, uncertain of our beau's affection. Obsessively, we look for signs. Making up stories, we torture ourselves, moving ourselves to tears with fantasies of his betrayal. We want the clue that will bring us certitude. We will not find it when our minds are locked in obsession.

Today, a student approached me on a teaching break. Her eyes were darting and her demeanor was nervous. "I have a question," she asked. "But I don't want to ask it in front of the class."

"Go ahead," I told her.

"How do you get an agent?" she asked quietly.

"Oh—that's a good question. I can give you the name of my agent. Do you have a manuscript you are sending out?"

"No, it's not finished yet. But it's going to be a book for young boys. I want to have the same agent as J. K. Rowling."

"I don't know who J. K. Rowling's agent is, but I think when you finish a piece of work, if it is ready, it does tend to find its next step." I could see that instead of spending her time finishing her book, she was spending her time obsessing about the future of a book that did not yet exist.

"I've tried Google, but I still can't figure out who represents Rowling," she said. She did not want to hear my questions about what her actual plans were for the manuscript.

"It's common for agents, especially the biggest ones, to keep a low profile," I told her. "But finding an agent can happen later. For now I think you should work on finishing your book."

"But you're my only chance," she said, getting irritated now.

"Why is that?"

"You're the only person I know who has an agent."

"I think your best chance is to start by finishing the book." But she did not want to finish the book. She preferred to obsess about a future that she was not actually taking steps to move toward.

"Work on your book," I pushed her. "I think that's the next thing for you to do."

"But can I ask you one more question?"

"What is it?"

"How much is standard commission for an agent to take? I don't want to get ripped off."

"To work with God-power, you must give it right-of-way and still the reasoning mind. The instant you ask, Infinite Intelligence knows the way of fulfillment. Man's part is to rejoice and give thanks, and act his Faith."
—Florence Scovel Shinn

Caught in a cycle of fantasy, wondering what our idea might be worth before we have the idea fully formed, is an avoidance of action, an avoidance of clarity in the moment. If we have decided that we need to be assured of success in order to start, we are giving ourselves permission to never start. Obsession is tricky; obsession is blinding. To move ahead, we must break the obsessive thought patterns that distract us from the good ideas we are working to form.

Cara was a successful businesswoman. The manager of a department, with many workers under her watchful gaze, she had a secure and lucrative job. Her work was appreciated, and she received many bonuses to ensure she stayed happily employed. Cara met Ted at a conference. He worked a parallel job to hers at a competing firm. Telling herself she had good boundaries, she embarked on a heady affair. It was a game to her at first, keeping her work secrets separate from her lover.

"I'm trustworthy," she told herself, but the question arose: Just how trustworthy was Ted? At times, he asked her too many questions. She was uncomfortable, but hid her discomfort, wanting to remain in Ted's good graces. Finally, she began to confide in Ted, trusting him with her corporate secrets. When Ted used the information to his benefit and her detriment, Cara was horrified. But she had only herself to blame. Her obsessive love had blinded her to Ted's motives.

But how do we break an obsession? The first step is admitting to ourselves that we are obsessed. Second, we must admit that we have an Achilles' heel that enabled us to be victimized. Third, we must look for our obsessive pattern. Fourth, we must tell somebody the truth of our situation. Fifth, we must be willing to let the Higher Power take us to better things.

Using the tools, Cara tried to step back from her situation. She knew she was obsessed with Ted. She fell asleep thinking of him and woke up having dreamed of him. She checked her BlackBerry compulsively, wondering whether he had texted her, reading into whether he had or hadn't. She read any communication from him over and over, studying his message, looking for subtext. She was distracted at work, distracted walking down the street. Cara was distracted, period. And her obsession was now getting her in trouble.

Looking at her history, Cara recalled two other times when she had trusted a man too soon. Somehow she "spilled the beans" too easily when she felt infatuated by someone. Whether it was about her work, her personal history, or her family, she often had experienced a quiet voice asking, "Am I saying too much?" when she was still early in a relationship, still getting to know her lover. And now here she was again, officially obsessed, and paying for it with her emotional instability and her careless behavior at her job.

Cara was angry at herself. As she saw her situation more clearly, and saw that she had put herself in this position before, she realized that it wasn't only Ted's fault that she was compromising herself at work. Yes, Ted had taken advantage of the information she had given him. No, Ted wasn't really trustworthy. But Cara had given the information away freely. Dismayed, Cara saw that *she* was the one she didn't trust.

Cara called a close friend whom she had known since childhood. She told her everything. Cara recalled how, when they were in second grade, she helped a boy cheat on a test—and got caught. "I was giving away my answers, even then," Cara said, now laughing at herself. "The pattern is so obvious once I see it. I hope I can learn."

"I saw my Lord with the eye of my heart, and I said: Who art Thou? He said: Thou."

—AL-HALLAJ

Letting herself share openly with her friend, Cara felt lighter. Hoping to learn from her mistakes, Cara was indeed asking the Higher Power for help. Not religious, Cara didn't have a God she prayed to—but through her honesty and correct intention, she *was* praying—and positioning herself to let go of that which no longer served her. Eventually, she distanced herself from Ted and repaired the damage at work. But the biggest repair was on her own psyche. "I really hope I see this coming next time," Cara says. "It's much too painful. I really don't want to put myself through this again."

I suspect that Cara will indeed "see it coming" next time. Willing to do the work on ourselves, we heal ourselves in the present and protect ourselves in the future.

IN GOD'S TIME

The prosperous heart is farsighted. Rather than settle for shortsighted goals, we aim always for the longer view. Asking for God's will for us, we are sometimes given glimpses of our future. "So that's where we're going!" we think. The future is often brighter than we'd dare to hope. "Trust me," God seems to be saying. "I have your best interests at heart." Our best interests may often surprise us, but the prosperous heart is flexible, able to take in God's agenda rather than stubbornly insisting on its own. The prosperous heart is curious. "Let's see where God is taking us," it begins to think. Members of twelve-step programs pray daily for knowledge of God's will and the power to carry it out. When their prayer is answered they often exclaim they are living a life beyond their wildest dreams. The prosperous heart is expansive. It expands to encompass God's plans for us.

Libby had always wanted to write, but until her painting arm was injured, she never found the time. Injured, she found her way to greater creative health. "No matter what becomes of my memoir, I had a wonderful time writing," says Libby. "My readers are encouraging. I may even have a talent."

"I may even" often points to God's will for us. God's will for us is oftentimes different from—and better than—what we had in mind. For Libby, painting for a living was already a dream come true. She never dreamed that she could add in writing, but when God urged her in that direction, she cooperated. Rather than fret about time lost while she couldn't paint, she looked for inspiration about how she might spend her time instead. The prosperous heart is available for God's agendas.

With practice, we learn to listen to—and cooperate with—the hunches that come to us. When we get a glimmer of where God intends us to go, we willingly go in that direction. We do this even if that direction may strike us as unlikely. Music was the unexpected direction that God chose for me. Writing my Morning Pages, three pages of longhand morning writing intended to guard and guide me, I was told I would soon be writing "radiant songs." This struck me as unlikely. I had been raised as the nonmusical member of a large and musical family. Surely if I were musical, I would know it. After all, at the time I was forty-five years old! I was skeptical, but willing to obey. Sitting by the side of a creek in the Rocky Mountains, I heard my first song. I raced to record it. It was, indeed, "radiant"—just as I had been told. It is now fifteen years since I heard that first song. Songwriting has become matter-of-fact for me. I now routinely sit at the piano and pick out melodies. I have written two albums of children's songs and three musicals, a note at a time.

"Impossible," I would have told you, yet all I had to do was cooperate. I bought a tiny keyboard and labeled the keys alphabetically, G to G (I remembered that much from abortive childhood piano lessons). I would hear a note, pick it out on the keyboard, and then write it down. I soon had an alphabetical code of the song. Next I bought children's notation paper and, with the help of a music student, translated my letters into notes. Voilà! Music!

Suzanne is a successful businesswoman and an inspired jewelry designer. "I believe that God never wastes our time," she says, "no matter how slow we *think* He is going. If we are waiting, we can assume God is working on the other players in our situation. Always.

"May there be the abundance of grain in the land; on the tops of the mountains may it wave; may its fruit be like Lebanon; and may people blossom in the cities like the grass of the field."
—Psalm 72:16

I can look back over sixty years and I cannot find a time that this hasn't proved to be true—eventually, anyway." Suzanne's faith is reassuring. Her career and her body of work both display every sign of success. She is active, daily, on behalf of all of her projects. But her temperament is gentle. She takes the action, but lets go of the result. And this brings her peace. "The one thing I know is that I'm not in control." She laughs. "Thank God."

The prosperous heart has a gentle, steady pace. We do not rush, agitated by feelings of urgency. We allow events to unfurl. We meet each day's happenings with grace. We ask for a proper understanding of events as they unfold. We ask for knowledge of God's will for us and the power to carry it out. We do not run pell-mell. We are temperate.

"Form a vacuum for prosperity, by cleaning up and cleaning out."
—CATHERINE PONDER

WEEK EIGHT CHECK-IN

Morning Pages: Did you do them this week? How many days?

Counting: Did you count this week? What did you learn?

Abstinence: Did you abstain from debting this week? If you did debt, what was it for? How did you feel?

Walking: Did you walk this week? What insights did you have?

Time-Out: Did you take your Time-Outs? What did you learn?

Prosperity Points

1. Set aside a small area for an altar. Gift yourself with fresh flowers, a candle, a seashell or pinecone, something that speaks to you of abundance and beauty. Building your

altar requires you to slow your pace and pay attention. Just as you can't rush a flower to open, you can't force your own insights or rush your unfolding process. Pausing to honor the sacred dignity of all life, we bless and savor each moment as it passes, seeing that everything is unfolding perfectly in God's timing.

2. What have you been putting off until tomorrow that you could start in some small way today? Fill in the following sentence ten times:

   1. I could _____

   2. I could _____

   3. I could _____

   4. I could _____

   5. I could _____

   6. I could _____

   7. I could _____

   8. I could _____

   9. I could _____

   10. I could _____

3. We all have patterns we fall into, and we all have weaknesses. We may suspect we know what ours are. Fill in the following sentence:

   1. I seem to have a weakness for _____

   2. I seem to have a weakness for _____

3. I seem to have a weakness for _____

4. I seem to have a weakness for _____

5. I seem to have a weakness for _____

4. Set aside twenty minutes and write about an obsession. What or whom are you obsessed with? Have you been obsessed with a similar thing or person before? Who is a safe person to share this with? When we are honest with another, we open the door to healing.

5. Number from one to three. List three instances in which you followed God's guidance in an unexpected direction and had the result work out wonderfully.
   1. When I moved to Chicago and shot a feature film there.
   2. When I loved Mark despite his status as a confirmed bachelor. (We got married.)
   Etc.

Now, describe one situation where you are impatient with how slowly your plans seem to be progressing. Ask for the grace to accept God's timing instead. Remind yourself that the universe is unfolding exactly as it should. There are more variables than you can see. Accept God's timing as being for the highest good for all.

Week Nine

GENEROSITY

By this point in the course, faith and serenity are feelings you are becoming familiar with—even accustomed to. This is the sign of a prosperous heart. As you feel a growing sense of trust in God and in yourself, you will desire to be more generous. God is generous with you, and in turn, you can be generous with yourself and others. This week you will explore the many ways in which generosity manifests itself in your life and think about how you can cultivate a generous spirit.

FRIENDSHIP

I am teaching a workshop in Virginia Beach at the Edgar Cayce Association for Research and Enlightenment. I enjoy coming here. The staff at the center is interesting and accommodating. My hotel room looks out onto the vast Atlantic Ocean. Edgar Cayce himself fascinates me. A psychic at the turn of the last century, Cayce conceived ideas that are still radical—and still in practice—a hundred years later. It seems incomprehensible, and yet the buildings he built are still standing, still housing his institute, which is still operating, still following his practices. There are Edgar Cayce centers in thirty-seven countries. My host proudly tells me that this center houses the second-largest metaphysical library in the world. "What's the largest one, then?" I ask her.

"The Vatican," she replies. "But it's hard to get in there."

My students in Virginia Beach are open, educated, inquisitive. The time flies by, even with a rigorous workshop schedule. But I have a secret: my favorite part of coming to Virginia Beach is seeing my friend Tim Farrington, who lives here year-round.

I am on the record—many times over—as saying that Tim is my favorite author. His *New York Times* Notable Book *The Monk Downstairs* inspired my own novel *Mozart's Ghost.* I had admired him from afar until a mutual friend met him and, in her charmingly pushy way, asked him to sign a book for me, only to discover that he was a fan of my work, as well. We contacted each other and became fast friends—and have been ever since.

Living far apart, Tim's and my relationship exists mostly through e-mail. Still, I count him among my closest beloveds. Seeing him in person fills my heart with joy. "I have so many questions," he says, hugging me. "Tell me everything. I want every detail." And I feel the same. With Tim, conversation always runs deep. We share many levels of experience, both of us having shown up at the page, daily, for nearly four decades now. Finding friendship with someone whose creative path parallels our own is a rare gift. I tell him as much.

"We do have a 'twinship,'" he muses. "Indeed. I think it's that we both cherish the process. And if you're going to be a writer, you'd better cherish the process, right?" His eyes spark with mischief and his dimpled smile comforts me. Tim has for years risen four hours before "everyone else" to get his writing time in. Today, with teenagers in his house up at five thirty, he rises mighty early.

"Today I got up at one thirty," he affirms.

"Wow." I was barely falling asleep by one thirty.

"But I have to do it," Tim says, as simply as one might state that they need to drink water or breathe fresh air to stay alive. I know exactly what he means.

"I still do Morning Pages every day," I tell him. "I'm betting on them."

He nods. "I know. I've always related so powerfully to that. It's your spiritual practice."

"It is," I say. "And I trust that if I keep doing them, I'll be guided to the next thing."

He studies me. "What is the next thing, do you think? After this book?"

"I don't know."

He lights up. "So you'll go to your windowed writing room in Santa Fe and find out."

"Yes, I suppose I will." I smile.

Looking for what is next—what God has in store for us—is an approach that Tim and I share. Sometimes, in between projects, my Morning Pages serve "just" as praying on the page. But praying on the page is what has always led me to my next work. For Tim, the process is similar.

"I know how to write another novel," Tim says. "But I have always let myself be moved to write as well. I don't want to just 'grind' away, even though I could. Sometimes, lately, I find myself just praying."

I understand. It is always a balancing act—moving ahead while letting the flow go where it will—as opposed to where *we* will *it*. For my part, I leave my visit with Tim inspired. The friends in our lives with whom we can share our deepest selves freely are often our greatest source of strength. We thrive in the company of kindred spirits, those friends who "get" us completely, whose values and lives are so in sync with our own that we can go weeks or months without seeing one another, but pick up right where we left off when we do connect again. Our closest friends are truly our greatest gifts.

Last week, in New York, Emma and Tyler staged a reading

"It is not because things are difficult that we do not dare; it is because we do not dare that they are difficult."

—SENECA

of their new musical, *Blue,* a story about a rare blue lobster—a real, one-in-two-million occurrence. Today Emma is traveling to Chicago, where they will stage another reading at the end of the week.

"I think we're making good progress," she declares. I attended the New York reading and listened with interest as Emma and Tyler discussed their process. Less than two years into their collaboration, they have a shorthand with each other and a palpable chemistry. Charging ahead daily, they appear to be unstoppable, moving at a dizzying pace and never at a loss for energy or ideas.

An actor at the reading of *Blue* watches their interaction with each other.

"Do you guys always agree on everything?" he asks.

They both laugh. "No," they say in unison.

"But we always listen to each other," Emma says.

"We trust each other completely. If one of us is concerned about anything, we stop until we both understand what it is," Tyler chimes in.

"Yes. If Tyler senses something that I don't see yet, that's enough for me to know that we need to stop and look closer."

"When we met, we knew immediately that we would be friends," Tyler adds. "And our friendship has always been the most important part of our relationship."

I am happy that Emma has found a kindred spirit. Watching them together, with their quick smiles and mischievous banter, I see that their joy in having found each other is obvious. I think of Tim's words about cherishing the process. It is clear that they do. Even though this reading of *Blue* exposed more work that needed to be done, they jumped in enthusiastically. With no interest in engaging in writerly drama, they are already well into the next step, sitting next to each other on the piano bench, working through their ideas.

With a healthy work relationship based in a deep friendship, they seem destined to accomplish great things together.

Looking out across the water from my hotel room, I wonder whether there is a blue lobster in its depths, searching for her soul mate. I hope she will find the companionship and understanding that Emma finds with Tyler, that I find with Tim.

The prosperous heart is communicative. Rather than stewing in anxiety, the prosperous heart reaches out to friends. Getting current with someone who loves and understands us yields an overall sense of well-being.

BEING GENEROUS

Generous is defined as "liberal in giving or sharing." To feel truly prosperous, we must find a balance; the place where we are comfortable with the flow of our money and energy. We are not miserly with ourselves or others. We are not spendthrift, either. Instead we strike a happy middle ground. We do not over- or underspend. We are balanced. We have an inner security that cannot be rocked by outer events. Esteeming ourselves, we find we also gain the esteem of others. Claiming God as our source, we are not thrown by worldly events. At all times, in all circumstances, we can depend on a Higher Power for support. Our emotional coffers are full.

"Every end is a new beginning."
—Unknown

Tomorrow, Sunday, I will call my friend Elberta. She is the matriarch of a paving empire and has as her avocation a flourishing horse farm where she raises award-winning Morgan horses. Possessed of a prosperous heart, she lives life to the fullest. Eighty-five years old, she has in the past half decade traveled to Russia, Australia, and Antarctica with her extended family in tow. Elberta's passion and enthusiasm characterize all of her encounters. She flings open the door at the farm, welcoming strangers and friends alike. There is always an extra place set at her table. A wonderful cook, she has a bountiful rhubarb patch, as well as an orchard. Visitors dine on her specialties: green chili stew and homemade pie.

Elberta takes me to the barn so I can see a newly dropped foal, Shazam, and a barn full of regal show horses. Although the mare is bay and the sire is bay, Shazam is bright chestnut. And in temperament, he is as bold and magical as his name suggests. Accompanying us on the tour of the barn is Anton, a gentle Doberman pinscher. Our guide is Elberta's daughter, Debbie Seybold, horse trainer par excellence. In the tack room stands a large loom. On it are two rugs, also the handiwork of Debbie. A magician with horses, a many-times-over national champion, she has a magic touch at the loom, as well. The rugs are made of cotton, but she also makes saddle pads out of wool. Although she has been weaving for only four years, she already enjoys a reputation as a master craftsman. Elberta is proud of her daughter and admires one rug in particular—a bright crimson glory. Debbie accepts the compliments lightly, moving us on through the barn.

In the back of the barn, in a cozy stall, I survey a rowdy flock of chickens—black, orange, and particolored—playing hide-and-seek amid the hay. The rooster, a tall, colorful bird, sounds his cock-a-doodle-doo and herds his hens from point to point. "Anton killed a chicken," Debbie notes. "I tied the dead chicken to his collar and made him spend the day with it. That cured him of killing chickens. Watch your fingers," she warns, as I stroke the velvet muzzle of Grand Opening, a prize stallion.

"He nips?"

"Yes, he nips."

"But he's so beautiful."

"And he knows it."

Grand Opening preens before the admiring women. He is the sire of little Shazam.

Debbie's generous spirit is much like her mother's. Our generosity does not have to be financial to be memorable and important. Simple hospitality is worth its weight in gold. Feeling welcome, our hearts prosper.

"Who is this one?" I ask, stopping by the stall door of a six-month-old filly named Scarlet. Scarlet arches her neck prettily, and gives her thick mane a quick toss. She is well named, a true femme fatale. Stopped at midstride, two quarter horses are tethered to the walker. Compared to the Morgans, they are plain Janes.

"They're ranch horses," Debbie explains. "They're named quarter horses because they're the fastest horse in the world for a quarter of a mile. They can spin on their hindquarters on a dime. They make fine reining horses."

Back at the house, Elberta's phone rings. She answers it quickly and her voice grows concerned. "I'll be right there," she tells her caller. Hanging up, she explains, "That's my friend Isabella on the line. She's ninety-two years old. She was calling to say she was dizzy. I'm going to drive over and check." With that, Elberta vanishes, her generosity needed elsewhere for the moment.

When I call Elberta, she always exclaims, "Julia!" as if I am her all-time favorite caller. Often when I call her it is to ask her for prayers. She has prayed me through many sets of rapids. Teaching, giving a speech—whatever the hurdle is—it is more easily conquered when she is praying for me. Elberta's prosperous heart anchors our friendship despite time and distance. "Julia!" she carols gladly, year in and year out. For my part, I have her daily in my morning prayers.

The first step toward generosity is prayer. Facing the day, writing a prayer to be guarded and guided sets the tone. A request to have knowledge of God's will and the power to carry it out puts the

"I live in an abundant universe."

—*DAILY WORD*

heart on the right footing. Sourced in God, acting in generosity is possible. The heart experiences a sense of abundance. An impulse to share God's largesse comes next, whether by giving of your time, your attention, your hospitality, or your money. The prosperous heart shares its bounty.

"It is your Father's good pleasure to give you the kingdom."

—LUKE 12:32

Uncompetitive, we know that God blesses all. No one else's good fortune can lessen our own. Neither does our own lessen that of others. We remind ourselves that God's stores are infinite. Thinking back over my own sobriety—thirty-three years now—I have learned over and over that the more I can share with others, the more my own heart prospers.

Recently I have been sharing books with a new friend. Finding something we think will interest or inspire the other, we pass it on. The latest book he has lent me inspires me again to be generous— with my assets as well as my stories.

A book of essays by recovering alcoholics, it contains harrowing stories about how their drinking dragged them lower and lower until they finally "hit bottom" and sought help. Seeking help, they found it, and their wasted lives were rescued. They all express gratitude, both to God and to fellow alcoholics, for giving them a second chance.

Many of the writers are now enjoying active and healthy lives. In their eighties or nineties, they find time to attend meetings with their fellow alcoholics and time to work with other alcoholics one-on-one. Across the board, they write of the joy of giving. Their lives have been transformed by helping transform the lives of others. Saved from a fate of jails, institutions, or death, they work to save others. Their prose bespeaks the joy they have felt helping others to avoid alcoholic catastrophe.

Before I know it, I am deep into the third story. This book grips me, offering the details of miraculous recoveries. The twenty story-tellers have recovered from a seemingly hopeless disease of mind, soul, and body. Their stories make clear that it has taken a spiritual intervention to halt their alcoholism. Time after time, the stories speak of desperate prayers that were answered. Lying in a back alley, "coming to" after a prolonged blackout, one writer begged for help—and his prayer was answered.

Another writer "came to" on Chicago's skid row, where he encountered a Catholic priest who urged him to seek medical help, which he did. Time and again the basic miracle of sobriety was reiterated. "I haven't found it necessary to take a drink or a drug for fifty-three years now." Time and again, the principle of one alcoholic helping another was put forth. Many of the writers have enjoyed happy marriages, living lives based on spiritual principles. The theme that runs throughout the book is the joy of living. Free from lives of a living hell, the writers were rocketed into a spiritual dimension. Giving to others, they found themselves being given lives filled with happiness and meaning.

As we give to others, we find our rightful place in the world. In rejoicing over the good tidings of our neighbors, our own self-centeredness slips away and we look to the future, believing in ourselves and our power to transform our lives through generosity toward others.

THE GENEROSITY OF THE UNIVERSE

My father harbored a prosperous heart. He had seven children and he was generous with each of them. As we settled into our adult lives, he gifted each of us with a down payment toward our first home. There were no strings attached to these gifts. His sole wish was to see his children flourish, and flourish we did, paying him back for his goodwill. The example set by a prosperous heart seems to call

"The all-providing substance of Spirit is everywhere present. I mold it with my thoughts and make it tangible with my faith. I am abundantly provided for."

—UNKNOWN

forth generosity in others. A generation after my father's gifts, we seven siblings are generous with one another, share and share alike.

I often sense that my father is proud, watching out for me and my siblings. I pray to his spirit for guidance, and many times have felt that the wisdom I have "heard" sounded very much like what my father might have said.

As I looked for my new home in Santa Fe, I thought of my father's generosity. I hoped that he would help me on my search—and indeed, it seemed as if he would.

As soon as I had decided that I would relocate, many things seemed to fall into place. I phoned Unity Church of Santa Fe and asked them if I could teach there. They were delighted to oblige me, and we settled on Sunday afternoons from two until four, starting within weeks of my arrival. Also through Unity, I was put in touch with a realtor, Lynne Murray, who helped me search for my ideal home. I had a long list of things I thought I wanted: an apartment, not a house; within walking distance of coffee shops and galleries; sunny, with mountain views; rent that was a third of my New York rent. Over the phone I liked Lynne. She seemed to listen carefully. Emma and I planned a four-day trip to Santa Fe to look at potential homes for me. Four days should be long enough for me to find something, I thought.

"You'll never find a hotel room for the dates you want," I was warned. "It's Indian Market and some thirty thousand tourists descend on Santa Fe. You might have to stay in Albuquerque!" I suggested to Emma that we get on the Internet and try for a hotel room in Espanola, the town my friend Elberta lived in. Sure enough, we found a suite halfway to Espanola. It was at the Buffalo Thunder Resort & Casino. We would ignore the gambling and use the suite as home base. Santa Fe was twenty minutes to the south.

Early in the morning on my first day in town, we met Lynne and set about house hunting. The very first place she showed me had everything on my list. The problem was, I hated it. Next we set out to view a series of "almost everything on your list" places. We quickly eliminated half of them because they featured white carpeting, a recipe for disaster, I knew from my years living in Taos. The red New Mexico dirt made for a gooey mud that quickly tracked up pale carpeting. We looked at one house that was very glamorous. It featured a laundry room, a study with built-in bookshelves, commanding mountain views, and beautiful gardens. It also featured several large murals and floors with inlays that were polished to a high gloss. "What do you think?" Lynne asked. I answered, "I think I would kill the gardens, and I would feel like I was living in someone else's trophy house. It all but shrieks, 'See how successful I am!'"

Lynne thought for a moment. "I have a crazy idea," she said. "I don't know why I'm taking you to this next place—but let's try it." We traveled to a smaller, more modest house tucked away in the piñon trees. The vacating tenant had four kids. The yard was strewn with toys. The inside of the house was all a-jumble. Couches blocked doorways. Clothes festooned chairs. You had to squint to make out the fact that the house was actually charming and featured a large multiwindowed room perfect for writing. "I like it," I told a startled Lynne. "I'll take it." The house was nestled in the foothills, several miles from galleries and coffee shops. It wasn't particularly sunny. It featured no mountain views. And it was a house, not an apartment. But the writing room jutted straight out into the trees, and I would be able to hang bird feeders in a semicircle. It was a house my father, a birder, would have loved.

"The more you depend on forces outside yourself, the more you are dominated by them."

—Harold Sherman

September 1 was the day slated for packing. September 2, the movers would load the truck. Emma and I would drive cross-country with my dog, Tiger Lily. Our goal was to arrive in Santa Fe before my belongings. The moving company called to say they would be ready to unload September 6. Emma and I arrived at twilight September 5, and this time we found a Holiday Inn Express not far from my future home. As she had the whole trip, Tiger Lily settled in peaceably. At eight a.m., we would meet the movers.

We got to the house at seven thirty. True to their word, the landlady and landlord had cleaned the house and done away with all of the rubble. We stepped over the threshold into a charming domain. Now if only my furniture would fit. The movers arrived at eight sharp. I began pointing them here and there. My furniture fit as if it had been designed for the little house, sometimes with only inches to spare.

"Put it there," I would say.

"It won't fit," the mover would reply.

"Try it," I would insist.

"I'll be damned!" the mover would exclaim.

I smiled to myself, remembering my father's stubborn confidence in his own ability to determine where furniture would best go. He didn't give up easily when he had a vision for a room, and neither would I. And so it went, piece by piece, until the house was snugly furnished. What remained to be fitted were boxes full of files. As I looked at the boxes, my heart sank. It would take me months to unpack them. I said as much to Emma.

"I'll do them," Emma replied.

True to her word, Emma began early the following day, and by nightfall every last box was unpacked. "You're a miracle worker," I told her. Unpacked and organized, the house was charming. I felt glad I had taken the modest little house and not any of the others that had actually met my specifications.

"It suits you," Emma declared.

"I think it does," I answered. "It's a house my father would have chosen."

And maybe he did.

Two brief days passed, and Emma headed back to New York. The house felt empty at first without her. I went to buy bird feed-

"I am aware of the Divine within me. Peace, quiet and confidence flow through my thought."
—ERNEST HOLMES

ers at a store called Wild Birds Unlimited. I selected three feeders for small birds and another larger feeder for blue jays.

"Most people don't want jays," the saleslady advised me. "They feel they chase away smaller birds."

"If they have their own feeder?"

"They like unshelled peanuts."

"I'll take a big bag."

"If you say so."

And so I outfitted the piñon trees skirting my writing room. The three feeders for small birds began immediately to do a brisk business. Chickadees, nuthatches, and juncos swooped to the feeders, hanging upside down to eat their fill. Next came the jays, balancing on their own feeder to chow down on peanuts. As long as their own feeder featured peanuts, they ignored the other feeders and the little birds they attracted. I felt triumphant. Then again, maybe the intuition on jay wrangling came from my father, too.

When we look at our history as a history of answered prayers, we experience a sense of optimism and confidence. We expect each new entreaty to add another jot to our abundance. God is inclined to say yes to us, we believe. We know that it is God's nature to give and our own nature to receive. God is energy, pure creative energy. We are God's creations and are intended to further God's creativity through our own. Asking God to extend to us a blessing is asking God to fulfill his own nature. This causes both human and divine joy.

"God supplies all that I need, when I need it, and I am open and receptive to my good."
—Unknown

WEEK NINE CHECK-IN

Morning Pages: Did you do them this week? How many days?

Counting: Did you count this week? What did you learn?

Abstinence: Did you abstain from debting this week? If you did debt, what was it for? How did you feel?

Walking: Did you walk this week? What insights did you have?

Time-Out: Did you take your Time-Outs? What did you learn?

"I learned that the real creator was my inner Self, the Shakti. . . . That desire to do something is God inside talking through us."

—MICHELE SHEA

Prosperity Points

1. Take the time to contact a beloved friend. Communicate how and what you are doing. Listen to your friend's update as well. The prosperous heart counts good friends among its greatest riches.

2. Fill in the following sentences:

    1. I could be generous by _____

    2. I could be generous by _____

    3. I could be generous by _____

    4. I could be generous by _____

    5. I could be generous by _____

    6. I could be generous by _____

    7. I could be generous by _____

    8. I could be generous by _____

    9. I could be generous by _____

    10. I could be generous by _____

Now, take pen in hand and recall a time when you were able to be generous, placing helping others ahead of your own desires. How did you feel afterward?

3. Take a moment to reflect, filling in the following sentences:
   1. Counting has made me feel like I have enough money.
   2. Counting has made me realize that I spend too much money on dining out.
   3. Counting has made me wonder whether I buy too many shoes.
   4. Counting has made me _____
   5. Counting has made me _____

   1. Abstaining, I feel _____
   2. Abstaining, I feel _____
   3. Abstaining, I feel _____
   4. Abstaining, I feel _____
   5. Abstaining, I feel _____

   1. Taking Time-Out, I _____
   2. Taking Time-Out, I _____
   3. Taking Time-Out, I _____
   4. Taking Time-Out, I _____
   5. Taking Time-Out, I _____

"Acceptance of what has happened is the first step to overcoming the consequences of any misfortune."

—WILLIAM JAMES

1. I have felt the generosity of the universe when _____

_____

2. I have felt the generosity of the universe when _____

_____

3. I have felt the generosity of the universe when _____

_____

4. I have felt the generosity of the universe when _____

_____

5. I have felt the generosity of the universe when _____

_____

4. Recall and describe one answered prayer. Allow yourself to feel your gratitude and joy. Write a brief prayer thanking God for this blessing.

"God, I am grateful for your help with my novel *Mozart's Ghost*. Thank you for your help with my discouragement. Thank you for giving me the strength to keep on making submissions. Thank you for Marcia Markland, a first-class editor. Thank you for the grace of our collaboration. . . ."

Calling to mind the times when God has come through on our behalf helps to give us faith that God will indeed answer our prayers. As the great spiritual teacher Ernest Holmes phrases it, "If God answers our prayers today, why would he not answer them tomorrow?"

Week Ten

STAYING
ON COURSE

This week you will dig deep, looking closely again at your finances and where your actions and attitudes about money serve you—and changing the ways in which they do not. You will recommit to Counting and, in addition to thinking about how you spend your money, think about how you spend your energy—and how you are compensated for it. We go back to basics this week, looking at practical solutions for the challenges we face.

ASKING FOR MONEY

In our culture and in our families, talking about money is often seen as taboo. Our parents' incomes are not discussed. Whether our family has more or less money than the neighbors is something we wonder but don't ask—and when we do ask, we are often answered with discomfort and ambiguity. But talking about money pales in comparison with *asking* for money. And asking for money is an important thing that we must learn to do.

As we count, we begin to take stock of our "money in." Is it a steady stream, is it a mere trickle, or does it come in fits and spurts? Do we have to do anything to earn our money, or is it something that just appears in our bank account—a trust fund or an allowance?

If we do earn it, how much of our time is devoted to keeping the coffers filled? How much effort are we exerting? Are we being fairly compensated for our time and talents? And are we pouring our time and talent into work that is meaningful, or only working for a paycheck? We are ready now to speak up, ask questions, and assess how our time and energy relate to our income.

Rickey was a high school teacher who happily accepted a part-time job the year he graduated from college. Knowing how lucky he was to have a job in teaching at all, he energetically jumped into his work. Rickey was taking over a music position that had been filled by several different teachers over the last few years. The school was more focused on sports than on music, and Rickey saw enormous room for growth in the program.

Rickey began to spend long hours at school working to involve more students in music. He taught the two classes he had been hired to teach, but saw that in creating more performance opportunities for the students, he could spark their interest and educate them more fully. He started an after-school a capella group, which quickly became popular and filled up several of his afternoons. For the students who hadn't sung before, Rickey taught group singing lessons, adding more commitments to his schedule. Thrilled with the progress of his students, Rickey wasn't focused on counting his hours at work. He watched the choir grow and improve with pride.

Before long, the administration noticed the excitement in the music department and began asking the choir to perform at school events. Soon they were performing at outreach events, and neighboring schools had students auditioning to participate as well, even asking Rickey whether he could start a similar choir at their school.

Spending more and more time at school, Rickey often got home late at night and had to leave early in the morning to teach his classes. But finances were tight. Without time to work any other jobs, he was struggling to survive on what was still just a part-time teacher's

"God wants the best for us, always. With this in mind why should we worry about anything else?"

—EDWENE GAINES

salary. Looking at the hours he spent and the positive feedback he was receiving, he asked the dean for a meeting when it came time to renew his contract.

The administration and parents were thrilled with Rickey's contributions to the school in only one year, and his reviews were stellar. But although Rickey appreciated the compliments, he knew he had to speak up.

"What I am doing is full-time," Rickey explained, "but the position is part-time. So I think either the position needs to adjust, or I do—but I can't continue putting in full-time hours for a part-time salary, as much as I love the work."

To Rickey's surprise, the dean was immediately responsive. "We'll look into it," he promised. And a week later, the school had made Rickey a full-time teacher with full-time benefits.

"By using prosperity affirmations, you are not trying to make God give you anything. You are only trying to open your mind to receive the abundance He has already given you."

—Catherine Ponder

"I'm so happy I just asked," Rickey says. "I didn't know what they would say, but I also didn't want to start resenting the time I was putting in. The kids don't deserve that. So I spoke up—and it worked out. I can afford to keep going—financially and emotionally—with the new contract."

So often when we are being underpaid for our talents, we feel as though it is off-limits to speak up. We tell ourselves we are lucky to have anything at all, when in fact our employer may be very lucky to have us—and may even be quite receptive to our request. If we speak up calmly, before we are in a position of feeling resentful, we may avoid not only being taken advantage of, but also engaging in a confrontation that could risk the job we are depending on for our livelihood.

But what if a pattern of being undervalued is already established in our lives? How do we extract ourselves from a situation that is both ingrained and unfair?

"I'm sixty years old," says Sam, "and still financially insecure." An actor, Sam has worked as a freelancer his whole life. Sometimes his acting jobs pay well; often they do not pay at all. On the side, he started a photography business and also used his graphic talents to design Web sites.

"My acting jobs come when they come, but I can't count on that as a source of income," he says. "And I've been building Web sites for five hundred dollars when a buddy needs a break. But in Counting, I realize I've been earning about eight dollars an hour. I've been doing a lot of favors for friends—but I'm definitely not doing myself a favor."

Sam is correct: he's not doing himself a favor. And when we do the right thing for ourselves, it is also the right thing for the people in our lives. Enabling friends or colleagues by giving our services away doesn't really help us—or them. And it certainly doesn't help our relationships.

"Recently a guy told me he needed a free head shot and I just lost it," Sam says. "I know it's because of turning sixty, looking back and seeing how much I've given away. It's not about the head shot. It's about how I have run my financial life. When I give away my talent, what I'm really saying is that I don't value my talent."

It is important to keep tabs on our emotional well-being related to the jobs we are doing. That is not to say that we will never work for free, that being generous is counterproductive, or that we should go through the world demanding extravagant payment for anything we do. It is a balancing act, trying to find a place where we are comfortable with the terms of the exchange. It is up to us to speak up when the balance tips away from us. Whether our employer gives us a raise or doesn't, it is the act of standing up for ourselves that opens the door to self-worth and prosperity.

"See if I will not open the windows of heaven for you and pour down for you an overflowing blessing."
—MALACHI 3:10

WHEN WORK IS SCARCE

"But, Julia!" My friend wails. "I don't have a job. It has been six months. I can't just pray to have a sense of prosperity when I literally can't pay the bills."

"When we give, everyone is a winner."
—JOHN MARKS TEMPLETON

Of course not. And everyone has times when work is scarce.

When Nancy was in the midst of a painful and financially devastating divorce, she had very little money to care for her young son. Sometimes eating ramen noodles for supper with money out of the change pot, she struggled daily to make ends meet. She stayed in a friend's guesthouse as she got back on her feet. Eventually, she found work, paying her friend back for the rent he had waived at the time, and was able to create a stable environment for her son. She looks back on that time now with interest.

"At the time, I felt humiliated," she says. "I felt unloved and unlovable, and having to ask for help from friends was hard for me. I also had had a very luxurious lifestyle that I gave up in leaving my marriage. It was a shock on all fronts."

But Nancy more than survived that time—she even had some of her best ideas in that period. A writer, she found the experience rich with emotion, and it created strong characters in the movie scripts she wrote—and sold—from the loaned guesthouse. She fed herself and her son, a day at a time, and he remembers the time fondly. "I still love ramen noodles," he says. "They remind me of gratitude, somehow."

Feeling humiliated at our time of financial instability or job loss is common. It is also very close to an emotional state that is our most valuable: humility. Humble, we are open to guidance. Humble, we are open to our own best ideas. Humble, we are in touch with our vulnerabilities, with the most human and sacred part of ourselves.

This is not to say that we want to be poor, or that things aren't easier when we are feeling more flush. But even in lean times, there are gifts to be received. There are lessons to be learned. There is a way out. As we continue to count, however small the numbers are, we keep ourselves grounded in reality and are able to focus our energies on seeking work to cover our necessities. No, it may not be our dream job, or even close, that we take in this time. It may be a job we never imagined ourselves doing. But as we take steps toward solvency, however small, we become courageous. We *do* prosper.

As adults we feel more shame about seeking money than children do. My next-door neighbor has a seven-year-old daughter named Tegan. Blond, athletic, and beautiful, Tegan is a force of nature, tearing down the driveway on her bike, climbing trees in the yard, always up for a challenge, and always encouraging her friends of all ages to join her in her adventures. Yesterday, she visited me early in the morning, her brown eyes fierce with determination.

"I'm playing the Money Hunt," she announced. "Can I play at your house?"

"The Money Hunt?" I smiled at her, wondering whether she could possibly know I was writing a money book. I could hardly wait to hear what the "Money Hunt" was.

"Yes," she said confidently, holding out her hand to expose two shiny dimes and a few pennies. "I found this at my house."

Tegan's mom, Pam, appeared behind her, looking at me questioningly. I nodded to Pam, letting her know that they both were welcome.

"The Money Hunt is where you go through the house hunting for money," Tegan continued. "You have to look in unusual spots: underneath cushions, in the bottom of the hamper, on the floor of the car, places like that. You can't go in pockets or purses. But you get to keep what you find."

"Oh, Tegan," Pam said. "We only do that at home. You don't ask other people—"

"Laying aside every sense of burden or false responsibility, losing all fear and uncertainty from my thought, I enter into my kingdom of good today."

—Ernest Holmes

"Come on in," I said with a laugh. Pam winked at me as she slipped in behind Tegan, who charged ahead with glee.

"I'll keep an eye on her," Pam said under her breath. "This will be quick."

I watched as Tegan explored my couches, looking between the pillows for treasure. Her agile hands were quick, and before long she discovered something.

"A big one!" she shrieked, holding up a quarter.

"It's yours." I smiled.

"Okay, Tegan, let's go now," Pam chided. They went on their way, Tegan beaming. I watched her, thinking that she felt like the richest girl in the world. And she is.

When we are willing to look for money in unusual places and let the optimistic and childlike part of us lead the way, we are likely to find a treasure, indeed.

"All who joy would win must share it—happiness was born a Twin."
—Lord Byron

COMPETITION AND JEALOUSY

One of the most potent obstacles to our financial and creative prosperity is the biting emotion of jealousy. "His car is bigger than mine," we think. "Her house is prettier." "I wonder how much those shoes cost; I wonder how much he has in savings; I wonder . . ."

As long as we are focused on another, we do not have our own full attention. As long as we are focused obsessively on the outer trappings of someone else's financial success, we are comparing our insides to their outsides—and that is never fair. Jealousy will *always* block our own prosperity—spiritual as well as financial.

Steve is a classical composer. Highly trained and intellectual, he is part of an elite group of writers—and he loves to remind everyone of that. Steve has had his works premiered in important places, performed by hot talents. But he has never made much money for his endeavors. "I'm a critical success," he says, and often. "That's more important than being a popular success."

Steve's defensiveness is rooted in his feelings toward his college roommate, also a composer, who went on to score many major movies. His college roommate now has multiple homes, steady income from his many projects, past and present, and a slew of impressive awards. And Steve is very jealous.

"He sold out," Steve mutters. "Being a commercial success isn't the goal. The goal is art." But it is Steve who is bitter. His colleague's career is a happy one, and the composer in question has nothing but praise for Steve's work. He also has no idea that Steve speaks so bitterly behind his back.

"I'm a better musician than he is," Steve says to anyone who will listen—while the world is listening to the music of his former roommate. Steve is trapped in a vicious cycle. The more he focuses on his friend, the more he is "losing" the competition. But there is no competition. Steve is simply making excuses for his own stalled career.

Looking more closely at Steve's work life, one can see that Steve is often "in between projects," meaning that he is taking a break from writing to talk instead about the injustices in the music world. Steve's bitter jealousy is actually a mask for procrastination. To hear him tell it, the world is against him. But look closely at his productivity, and he is the one slowing his own pace.

When we are focused on the competition, we are avoiding an action we need to take for ourselves. When we are jealous of another, we are probably avoiding a part of ourselves. Focused on our neighbor's car, we forget to wash our own. Focused on another's publishing success, we stew in resentment instead of writing another page of our own project. We must be gentle with ourselves in these moments. We are avoiding ourselves because we are afraid. We are

"Everyone and everything around you is your teacher."

—KEN KEYES JR.

afraid that, even if we were to give it our all, our all won't be enough, that we're second-rate, that God's will is for us not to be as successful and acclaimed as the person we are fixated on.

God's will is for us to be fully, completely, prosperously ourselves. *We* are the treasure we are seeking. But until we focus our gaze squarely upon ourselves and redirect all those jealous energies toward our own projects, we will never find the pot of gold.

"God is the constant, abundant source of my supply."
—UNKNOWN

DEVICES OFF

Even when we are not competing with other people, we can often feel like the world around us is competing for our time, money, and attention. When I published *The Artist's Way,* one of the most resisted—and most productive—tools in the book was one called "Reading Deprivation." Reading Deprivation is just what it sounds like: no reading. It casts us back onto ourselves, puts us in touch with our own thoughts and ideas, and often frees up a *lot* of time.

Today, when I teach this tool, I have updated it to include the many other pulls on our time and attention. The tool is now called "Media Deprivation." Cutting out reading alone is not enough. We are now bombarded with e-mails, texting, TV, radio. We carry devices in our pockets—and those devices carry the expectation that we are constantly reachable, for our jobs or for any reason. No longer is the evening respected as sacred family time. We are a twenty-four/seven society, and the iPhone dinging in our pocket pulls us out of our lives and our focus twenty-four hours a day.

For one week, I ask you to experiment with turning all devices off. This still includes no reading. But it also expands to include no e-mailing, no texting, no searching the Internet. No talk radio, no TV. And yes, I can feel the protests as I type this.

"But, Julia, I have an important job. I *have* to check my e-mail.".

"I work for a TV station. I *have* to watch the news."

"If I don't respond to my daughter's text immediately, she'll think I don't care."

Yes. I know. When I teach, I always say that "I teach adults." No, I am not asking you to quit your job or behave in a way that would get you fired. But, like that time in college when you procrastinated on a paper until the last minute, put off everything you can. For one week. And if you cannot push your work until tomorrow, you can certainly contain the access people have to you without being irresponsible. I am not asking you to be irresponsible to your work. I am asking you to be responsible to yourself.

When we are constantly interrupted, we lose our train of thought. There are endless studies about how we are not able to multitask— in actuality, we really can do only one thought-requiring action at a time. There are countless tragic stories of car accidents, train accidents, ferry accidents caused by the driver texting behind the wheel. We know this. We have nearly stepped into traffic ourselves once or twice when we hear the "ding" of an e-mail in our pocket and believe we must know who sent us something—*right now.* In all the ways you can, for one week, turn off your devices. If you must check them, set aside a short window of time where you will go and respond to what you must respond to. But challenge yourself with this. Is there any real reason that an e-mail needs to be responded to at seven p.m.? Can it wait until morning, until business hours?

You may find that when you turn off your devices, you feel uneasy in the awkward silence of "just" you and your own thoughts. But when we learn to engage in conversation with our own thoughts, we begin to find that we are enough. And when my students experiment with turning their devices off, they are often flooded with ideas. It is as if we are unblocking the dam for long enough to let the water flow through, rather than blocking the

"The only way to deal with the future is to function efficiently in the now."

—Gita Bellin

slightest trickle with a Google search of our own name because we are bored, checking the status updates of high school friends on Facebook, or immediately reading the offers in the e-mail that Domino's Pizza just sent us. Challenge yourself to stop all of this, cold turkey, for a week. You may well find you have no interest in turning it back on when you are finished.

Sharon was adamant that she would not do this exercise. "I can't," she told me. "I can't work if I'm out of touch. I don't want to miss anything. You're crazy if you think I don't need to check my e-mail."

"I didn't say you couldn't check your e-mail," I responded, feeling her deep waves of anger. "And I understand that this is a scary tool. I am simply asking you to severely limit your time spent this way."

When Sharon left the class that evening, I didn't think she would come back, much less try the exercise. Sharon was a classic iPhone addict. She often forgot to turn her phone off at the start of class, and when the sound of an incoming text message reminded her, she turned it to silent—not off. Anytime it vibrated, she looked at her device. She worked hard to look attentive to what I was saying as she quickly texted her reply. She checked her phone while other students were reading their work to her. She brought her phone into the bathroom with her. She had had three small fender-benders, all because she couldn't wait to see who the latest e-mail was from. She claimed that "her generation" could indeed multitask, and that she *was* listening, that she wasn't missing anything that was going on.

But to my eye, Sharon was almost *always* distracted. She would stop midsentence to check her phone, leaving the person she was talking to waiting. She would stop midstride to check her phone, blocking the people behind her on the sidewalk. She pulled her phone out during dinner with friends. She glanced at her messages during work meetings. And although she often frustrated the peo-

"Desire is the onward impulse of the ever-evolving soul."
—Charles Fillmore

ple she was (partially) interacting with, Sharon was sadly not very unusual.

When she walked into class the following week, I was shocked by her appearance. She had cut her hair and was carrying a brightly colored bag—also a new look for her. She wasn't looking at the phone in her hand or reaching into her purse to get the phone. She was looking me in the eye, smiling, and walking toward me with purpose.

"I did it," she said breathlessly. "I did it." Her eyes filled with tears as she sat down beside me. She was more alert than I had ever seen her.

"I turned the phone off, the computer, everything, for as much time as I could. At first I was so angry, but I thought, 'I'll do it for a week and then go back to however I want to be.' But I'm never going back to that," she said, looking down. "I realized this week that I have been the rudest person in the world. I couldn't have been more self-centered. I would go to a restaurant with a friend and check my phone during dinner. I wasn't listening to what anyone had to say because whatever e-mail had just come in—even when it was spam—was more important in that minute."

"Yes," I said to her. "We withdraw completely when we are distracted in that way."

"Now I watch people who do that—and lots of people do—and I feel so embarrassed. It's embarrassing to hold up an elevator full of people because I'm trying to finish a text and don't realize I'm blocking the door. It's so rude to bring five other friends to coffee with my brother when we are supposed to catch up. And that's what I'm doing when I'm checking my phone instead of listening to him. Every time I get distracted by my phone, I'm telling the person I'm with that I have something more important to do than be present to them."

Sharon reached into her bag and pulled out a stack of papers. "I wrote four songs this week," she said, blushing as she handed them to me.

"Because you could hear yourself think," I said gently.

When we focus ourselves, we come into who we truly are. When we schedule the time to check our e-mail, we are more efficient and accurate in our replies. Our sense of feeling scattered and overwhelmed dissipates as we control our devices rather than letting them into our lives at all hours. Like with the nosy, overbearing person who asks for too much from us, we must set boundaries with our devices, leaving ourselves to our own devices, and letting ourselves be present for our lives.

EDUCATION

One of the greatest ways we can increase our own value is to increase our education. Formally or informally, we all have something to learn, and are always able to gather more knowledge as long as we are willing to look for it. As Linus Pauling remarked, "Satisfaction of one's curiosity is one of the greatest sources of happiness in life."

My friend Mike is a case in point. A straight-A high school student, the president of his class, Mike dreamed of going to Harvard, and the dream seemed well within his reach until he got his girlfriend pregnant. Stripped of his honors—no longer class president—he was relegated to finishing high school in night school. There he fell in with a hard-drinking, hard-drugging crowd, and his dreams of Harvard went glimmering. In short order, Mike became a fullblown alcoholic. He dealt drugs as well. He was in a steady downward spiral until he encountered an insightful therapist. She recommended AA, and against all odds, Mike entered recovery.

A day at a time, he did the work of rebuilding his life. He entered college—not Harvard, but a well-thought-of school. He became an author, helping others by sharing his own trials and tribulations. All was well, but he still dreamed of Harvard and the bright life he could have had. One day it occurred to him he could still go to Harvard. He could enter a master's program. Heart in his mouth, he wrote to Harvard, telling about his early dream, his wreckage, and his reconstruction. Harvard accepted him for a master's in education. His dream of an Ivy League education became a reality.

The prosperous heart is humble, willing to rely on God. Mike asked God to guide his pen when he wrote to Harvard. He truthfully and humbly told his story. He did not posture. He wrote from his heart, and his letter was received in the spirit it was written. He acted in good faith, and his action was received in good faith. "It seemed miraculous to me," Mike says of his acceptance. And it was miraculous—just not to God. To the prosperous heart, such miracles become commonplace.

Theresa was a brilliant student, sailing through college and grad school. When she had children, she decided to stay home with them, instilling in them, too, the importance of education. But since she lived in a small town, Theresa's master's degree in art history had little to offer her in the job market. When her children both went to college, she decided to go back to school.

In her midfifties, Theresa went to the local college, obtaining a second undergraduate degree—but this time in computer science. "I was always good at math," Theresa muses. "I even have the nickname 'Computer,' because I can do a lot in my head very quickly. It's just how my mind works, I guess. But when I was in school, computer science didn't exist yet." Maybe, she thought, the timing was perfect. She attacked her classes, making friends with the other students, even working out with them in the gym. "I'm going to keep up with them," she announced to herself, and to everyone. And keep up she did. "I'm not going to the old people's classes at the fitness center. I'm going to the regular ones with my classmates,"

"At the darkest moment comes the light."
—Joseph Campbell

"I am not concerned about what happened yesterday. I know that today everything is made new."
—Ernest Holmes

she said stubbornly. Four years later, the valedictorian of her class, she had earned another bachelor's degree, and was hired to teach for a year at the very college she had just graduated from. A year after that, she got a job working for a major computer manufacturer.

"I got the best job of my life at fifty-eight," Theresa shares freely. Quickly promoted by the company and deeply respected, she is relied upon by her team. "I'm twenty years older than all of them and the only woman, but it's fun. I like my job."

Theresa has a prosperous heart. For the prosperous heart, the sky is the limit. When we pray and are led to actions that seem beyond our reach, we must remind ourselves: with God, all things are possible.

It is important to note that not everyone who is expanding their education can—or needs to—go back to college. Many times, we can educate ourselves without spending money or excessive amounts of time. Learning new skills can be very simple: joining a knitting circle, participating in a book club, taking a walking tour of your city to discover new neighborhoods.

Andy wanted to learn how to jog, but had never run "except for the bus" in his life. "I really didn't even know how to begin," he says. When he moved to Minneapolis for a new job, he joined a runners' club in his new city, hoping to get to know his way around. Every day he went out with a small group. At first they just walked. Then they walked faster. Then they alternated walking with light jogging. Then they did more jogging and less walking. Within a few weeks, he had jogged an entire lap around his local park. "I can't believe the sense of accomplishment," Andy says, elated. "Accomplishing this simple thing makes me want to set—and meet—more goals in my life."

When we take steps to educate ourselves in any way, large and small, we are filled with hope and energy. We always have the power to take *some* step forward.

WEEK TEN CHECK-IN

⁓

Morning Pages: Did you do them this week? How many days?

Counting: Did you count this week? What did you learn?

Abstinence: Did you abstain from debting this week? If you did debt, what was it for? How did you feel?

Walking: Did you walk this week? What insights did you have?

Time-Out: Did you take your Time-Outs? What did you learn?

Prosperity Points

1. Looking back through your employment history, has your compensation felt fair to you? When the pay was low, were there other benefits that made the job worth it? What about your employment today? Are you treating yourself fairly in your ratio of hours spent to dollars earned? Are you willing to speak up if you are not?

2. List ten people you are jealous of and why. Now look and see if there is an action you can take on your own behalf. Are you *really* as powerless as you think you are? Take one of those actions.

3. For one week, keep your devices off as much as possible. At the end of the week, reflect on what you found by doing this. Are you clearer, more in touch with yourself and your ideas? Do you feel that you will choose to keep distractions at bay in general?

4. List ten topics that interest you:

1. _____

2. _____

3. _____

4. _____

5. _____

6. _____

7. _____

8. _____

9. _____

10. _____

Fill in the following phrases:

1. I'd like to learn more about _____

2. I'd like to learn more about _____

3. I'd like to learn more about _____

4. I'd like to learn more about _____

5. I'd like to learn more about _____

1. I could educate myself by _____

2. I could educate myself by _____

3. I could educate myself by _____

4. I could educate myself by _____

5. I could educate myself by _____

1. A tiny action I could take is _____

2. A tiny action I could take is _____

3. A tiny action I could take is _____

4. A tiny action I could take is _____

5. A tiny action I could take is _____

5. Prosperity point: give yourself five minutes to write. Ask your inner seven-year-old what it thinks you should be doing to feel rich. The insights you hear may surprise you.

Look at your lists. Are there topics that show up more than once? Do you see areas that are clearly of interest to you? Is there a small action you can take in the direction of your interest? It is not necessary to overturn your life, go back to school full-time, or move to another city to study. The steps toward expanding your education can be small and gentle. It may seem old-fashioned, but the public library is a great place to begin to satisfy your curiosity. Online learning can be a convenient and affordable way to test the waters and see if you're really interested in a subject. If you're interested in learning a skill, ask around about whether someone in your community is an expert and might be willing to take on an apprentice. Or join a group of people who share a similar interest. Even the smallest step moves you closer to a prosperous heart.

PROSPERITY
AND OUR
DREAMS

This week you will explore your creative dreams, allowing yourself to acknowledge your desires and follow your impulses without letting money stand as an impediment. No matter how huge your dreams are or how expensive you may imagine them to be, there is always some action you can take right now, with your finances as they are, to explore your creativity and, in doing so, expand the joy in your everyday life.

OUR MONEY IS A MAP

If money were no object, what would you truly desire to do? This is a question well worth asking. We must stop automatically placing others' needs ahead of our own. What gives you joy? When we are joyful, others are drawn to us as never before. Working through the exercises and prosperity points of the week, we will discover many delights are well within our reach. We have simply been telling ourselves we can't afford them, that we don't deserve them, or that they're somehow inappropriate.

But why should we ask ourselves what we would do if money

were no object? If money were no object, we wouldn't have any problems, would we? And money *is* an object. Why indulge in fantasy? What good will that do us?

The answer is, a lot of good indeed. We often block our dreams with the excuse that we can't afford to accomplish them, when in fact we may well be able to take steps toward them.

"If money were no object, I'd cure cancer," Rich says.

Okay, so he can't do that, but what is this dream telling him? There are ways he can be of service in the medical field without spending money. He can volunteer in a hospital, go on a walkathon to raise money for a cancer organization.

Lindsay wanted to travel the world. "If money were no object, I'd be able to spend enough time in Barcelona to really know the city," she thought. "But it's too expensive to spend much time there. It's almost not worth going." Looking more closely at what she truly desired—time to explore—she looked again at her options of how to attain it.

"I realized I could use my frequent-flier miles for the plane," she says. "And I live in New York. That's a destination, too. Maybe someone in Barcelona wishes they could explore New York."

Six months later, Lindsay spent a month in Barcelona on a house swap. And the person who she swapped houses with became a close friend.

"Maybe we'll do this once a year," Lindsay muses excitedly.

"Beloved, I pray that in all things thou mayest prosper."
—3 JOHN 1:2

The trick is to look at our desire—what we *want,* rather than what we don't have or why we think we can't have it. With a little creativity it is often very possible to satisfy urges that seem at first glance to be out of our reach.

As we take small steps in the direction of our dreams, our dreams become more vivid and heartfelt. As Goethe said, "Whatever you think you can do, or believe you can do, begin it. Action has magic, grace, and power in it."

When we are obsessed with our financial insecurity, we lack the focus and clarity to pursue our dreams. As our money issues come into focus and we are able to ask for—and receive—divine assistance, so, too, are we able to accept the support of the universe for our dreams and wishes.

As we stop debting, we become able to receive abundance. As we build a solid base, we receive support from unexpected sources.

By now, you are familiar with your spending patterns. Counting is second nature. It is now time to look back at your spending patterns and your spending personality. What have you learned?

Calvin, a waiter, prides himself on his good looks and gentlemanly charm. In the oceanside restaurant where he works, he is the star. He listens to his guests, he helps the elderly women to their seats with ease and grace, and he earns the highest tips. His quick humor and intense focus make him popular and often requested.

Counting, Calvin discovered that he spent more money than he wished on clothes. He also saw his irrational belief that he couldn't afford to go to the movies.

"I buy socks that are more expensive than a movie ticket," he says. "I don't know what I am thinking, but I never let myself go to the movies."

His finances no longer mysterious to him, he began to dig a little deeper, looking at his creative assumptions and beliefs. Exploring his childhood dreams, he recalls getting the lead in the school play.

"I loved acting," Calvin says brightly. "I had so much fun doing that." But his father, a businessman, thoroughly instilled in his children the value of a job with a steady paycheck. Now working his way through business school, Calvin long ago dismissed any thoughts of acting. No wonder he won't let himself go to the movies. It's not about the ten-dollar ticket. It's far too painful to watch the acting he wishes he were doing himself.

Seeing clearly now the embers of the dreams that haven't quite died, Calvin decided to let himself explore acting again—*while* going through business school.

"I can audition for a play that rehearses at night," he says. "I can get my headshot and résumé together and send them out. It doesn't have to be either/or. I can go to business school and dip my toe back in the water of theater. And I don't need any more nice socks. I'm going to go to the movies once a week no matter what. Just for me."

Pursuing our dreams does not equal financial irresponsibility. When we see ourselves rejecting an idea because of money, we should be alert to look again at what we are assuming is impossible.

Money will not be the thing that sets your dream free. You will be.

THE NEXT RIGHT THING

There is only one action we ever need to take: the next one. Doing the "next right thing," we are always doing God's will. Doing God's will, we always have a prosperous heart.

The "next right thing" is usually something small. It may be finishing the essay—or the paragraph. It may be returning the call. It may be doing the laundry. The next right thing is not usually glamorous—in fact, the opposite. The next right thing is usually mundane, and it is always doable. It also always gives us a sense of satisfaction.

"The snow goose need not bathe to make itself white. Neither need you do anything but be yourself."
—Lao-Tse

How often have we fretted about a relationship for hours, when, in fact, what we needed to do was finish the report we were working on? In avoiding the report, we are creating drama—setting up a situation where we will have to rush to get it done or make an excuse for ourselves tomorrow, triggering feelings of guilt and self-attack. We know when we are not doing the next right thing, because the *actual* next right thing is bugging us, pestering us, dancing around our consciousness, tapping at our psyche.

Doing the next right thing, especially when that thing is small, takes courage. Doing the next right thing when people around us are dramatic or threatening takes even more courage. When we display humility and take the honest next step for ourselves, we are always rewarded with a sense of true accomplishment. Sometimes, the "next right thing" is as simple as "go to sleep."

When Pam was in college, she found that the hard-drinking antics of her classmates scared her. She retreated from the party scene, preferring to spend time with nondrinking friends, or alone. A creative writing major, she hoped to be published one day.

The head of her department was known for hosting parties at his house. With ample alcohol, even for the underage drinkers, his soirées were frequent and exclusive. Those students who were invited felt special, and the professor implied that being part of his social swirl would help them in their careers. An invitation to one of these parties was coveted by all—except for Pam. The scene made her nervous. As much as she needed help from her mentors, she couldn't believe that this was the way to get ahead. She declined the first invitation from her professor, who responded kindly. But when she declined the second invitation, her professor's demeanor changed abruptly. Sensing his disapproval, she was sure she had made a professional misstep. Still, she felt his parties were unethical, and continued to avoid them.

On Friday nights when her classmates were out partying, Pam stayed home. She would write a short story instead, and while she wondered whether she was "missing the action," she found satisfaction in the work she was accomplishing. At the end of college, Pam had not been to the exclusive parties—but she had written a short-story collection. She took the collection to her professor, who told her he could do nothing to help her.

Pam was crushed, and wondered whether she had made a mistake, whether she had not played her cards right. But she continued

"The influence of a beautiful, helpful, hopeful character is contagious, and may revolutionize a whole town."
—Eleanor H. Porter

to write, building her body of work. One day, working at a bookstore, Pam waited on a woman who piled three of Pam's favorite books onto the counter. Looking at the titles, Pam exclaimed in surprise, and they had a happy and fascinating conversation. The woman was clearly a kindred spirit.

"What do you do?" asked Pam.

"I'm a literary agent," the woman replied. "How about you?"

Pam blushed, suddenly nervous. When Pam admitted that she was a writer, the agent asked whether she had work that she would like to show her. Pam handed over the short-story collection. A year later, the agent—*her* agent—had sold it.

"I'm so happy that I wrote those stories," said Pam. "If I had focused on playing the game, I might still just be playing the game—with no work to show for it. Finding this agent is a dream come true for my career, but she's also become one of my closest friends. I'm grateful that I was willing to do the next right thing on my own instead of hanging out in the wrong company, trying to be cool."

Asking for guidance does not mean forsaking our free will. Rather, when we ask for guidance, our will is tempered. When we receive guidance and act on the suggestions that are made, far from erasing our individuality, obedience to God's will frees us to become more of ourselves. We are guided to dare to be original. We are, after all, the origin of our own actions.

"People need joy. Quite as much as clothing. Some of them need it far more."
—MARGARET COLLIER
GRAHAM

Acting in sync with God's will leaves us with a feeling of abundance. We know we have what we need. We may even have more than what we need. Sourced in God, we have an infinite supply of spiritual strength. Sourced in God, we are not lonely. We find God meets our needs and may furthermore meet our wants. We find that our will and God's will are not at opposite ends of the table. We have been praying for knowledge of God's will for us and the power to carry it out. Now we find our prayer has been answered.

NEVER TOO LATE

Jenna was in her fifties when she began taking my course. A photographer, she had done beautiful work for many years, but had kept it mostly to herself. Raising two sons, she assembled beautiful family vacation albums and shot artful portraits of her children that graced her thoughtfully decorated home. She taught photography part-time at a local high school, but rarely showed her work to anyone. Whenever people admired her home and her photography, she felt a combination of pride and sadness that perhaps she wasn't fully using her talents.

"One may become prosperous by building up a large thought about money, but he will not have the satisfaction that goes with true prosperity consciousness."
—MAY ROWLAND

When Jenna started Counting, she realized that she in fact had enough extra money, if appropriated correctly, to build herself a photography studio in the basement of her house. She completed it as her second son left for college. Suddenly left with time and freedom, she asked herself what she wanted to do.

"I had never been to the West," Jenna said. "I thought, 'What if I just go?' Ideally, I wanted to find a ranch, maybe photograph some horses, but I didn't know how I'd ever make that happen. So instead I just took my camera and went to Utah for a week."

When Jenna got to Utah, she traveled from small town to small town looking for subjects. An old five-and-dime store caught her eye. After taking pictures of the crumbling structure from every angle, she went inside.

"I went in to buy a Coke, and came out with a plan," she said. "I just asked anyone in the store whether they had a ranch, and someone did! And they said I could photograph whatever I wanted!"

Jenna's husband laughs, shaking his head. "When I got the call from her that she was about to follow some guy thirty miles into nowhere to photograph his horses, I really hoped it wasn't the last time I'd talk to her. I told her as much, but that certainly didn't stop her."

Jenna's journey into the woods of Utah would prove to be the beginning of her new career. Becoming close to the family that owned the ranch, she has gone back to visit and take photos for the last five years. She has published two books of her horse photos, and next week, a black stallion she photographed will be installed as a billboard.

"I really just followed my crazy idea," she said with a laugh. "I don't know. I just feel like it's my time."

And it is. The prosperous heart does not see age as a barrier to our dreams. In the moment of creation, we are timeless. As we follow our true passions, the ageless spark of our spirit takes hold. The prosperous heart is both young enough to adventure, and old enough to choose our adventures wisely.

The prosperous heart is flexible. It is able to go with the flow, shifting agendas as called for. Faith in the future makes change acceptable. The prosperous heart trusts that everything will work out for the best.

TIGER LILY'S ELK BONE

The moon is like a giant silver dollar tossed over the mountains. The piñon trees are nickel-plated. The dirt road to my house seems to glow in the dark. My headlights pick out the pewter chamisa bushes. It's been light at night for several days as the full moon waxes. Tonight is the climax. The moon is at its brightest.

I pull into my driveway, and through the glass doors of my little house I see Tiger Lily waiting and watching for me to come home. When I open the door, she dances a merry spiral, wagging her tail and yipping a hello.

For the better part of six months now, Tiger Lily has been eating a special diet of salmon, which she loves. I signal her into the kitchen by patting my hip. She knows this signal means, "Follow me; dinner is served."

In the back garden, two of the neighbors' dogs are pressed against the fence, barking. Their racket does not disturb Tiger Lily's focus on her dinner. At age thirteen, she is deaf and often sleeps through my arrival. Not tonight.

When I travel, Tiger Lily stays at a kennel called Paws Plaza. Leaving her, I must sign a waiver that she is allowed to chew bones. The kennel features several varieties for sale. I have discovered Tiger Lily's favorite is elk bones. She strongly prefers them to beef bones and to lamb. At night, as I try to drop to sleep, I hear a steady *click-click-click* as Tiger Lily chews on the evening's treat. A single elk bone will often last her several days, although sometimes she takes her treasure into the back garden, where she buries it for later retrieval.

Tonight she has decided to have an indoor meal. Perhaps the full moon is too bright for her sense of secrecy. She lies on the living room rug and turns the prize in one direction after another. The bone still has meat clinging to it—muscles and tendons. If I try to take the bone from her, she clenches it tightly in her jaws. She may go so far as to give a warning growl. She loves me, but not like she loves that bone.

And so I resign myself to the *click-click-click* of her passion. If I am lucky, she will remain in the living room rather than dragging her bone down the hall to my bedroom. Elk bones are a Western delicacy. I buy them in ten-dollar batches and store them in my freezer. I want Tiger Lily to be happy, and she seems on the whole to be pleased with her new habitat and her role as queen of the household.

I watch her, paws on the bone, tail wagging. She is focused and happy. I am struck by how satisfied she is with something so small. What can we learn from this? I wonder.

The prosperous heart allows itself small joys. Like Tiger Lily with her bone in the moonlight, it says, "I like this. This makes me happy. I have enough."

"That which I seek is seeking me. That which belongs to me will come to me. Since it is my desire that only good, truth, love, wisdom and power shall go from me, I know this is all that can come back to me."
—Ernest Holmes

WEEK ELEVEN CHECK-IN

Morning Pages: Did you do them this week? How many days?

Counting: Did you count this week? What did you learn?

Abstinence: Did you abstain from debting this week? If you did debt, what was it for? How did you feel?

Walking: Did you walk this week? What insights did you have?

Time-Out: Did you take your Time-Outs? What did you learn?

Prosperity Points

1. In exposing the dreams we have tried to ignore, it is common to feel overwhelmed. Go gently with yourself here. Small steps are all that are required.

   Fill in the following sentences:

   1. If I were younger, I'd _____

   2. If I were younger, I'd _____

   3. If I were younger, I'd _____

   4. If I were younger, I'd _____

   5. If I were younger, I'd _____

   1. If I were older, I'd _____

   2. If I were older, I'd _____

   3. If I were older, I'd _____

   4. If I were older, I'd _____

   5. If I were older, I'd _____

1. If it weren't too expensive, I'd _____

2. If it weren't too expensive, I'd _____

3. If it weren't too expensive, I'd _____

4. If it weren't too expensive, I'd _____

5. If it weren't too expensive, I'd _____

1. I still spend too much money on _____

2. I still spend too much money on _____

3. I still spend too much money on _____

4. I still spend too much money on _____

5. I still spend too much money on _____

1. I'd like to spend more money on _____

2. I'd like to spend more money on _____

3. I'd like to spend more money on _____

4. I'd like to spend more money on _____

5. I'd like to spend more money on _____

2. Take pen in hand and write a brief creative autobiography of your life. Allow yourself thirty minutes to put memories on paper, filling in the prompts below. How did you express yourself at different times in your life? Did you act in elementary school? Did you sing in the high school choir? Did you decorate your apartment in college? Large and small, your history of creative actions is a map of your creative life. Allow yourself to make connections as you write. What do you miss? What was fun? What have you denied yourself? What do you desire to do now?

Ages 0–5

1. I was aware of my creativity when _____

2. I wanted to _____

3. In my household, creativity was _____

4. I wished that I had _____

5. I was creative when _____

Ages 5–10

1. My creativity was _____

2. I felt creative when _____

3. I wanted to _____

4. In my household, creativity was _____

5. I wished that I had _____

Ages 10–15

1. My creativity was _____

2. I felt creative when _____

3. I wanted to _____

4. In my household, creativity was _____

5. I wished that I had _____

Ages 15–20

1. My creativity was _____

2. I felt creative when _____

3. I wanted to _____

4. In my household, creativity was _____

5. I wished that I had _____

Ages 20–present, in five-year increments:

1. My creativity was _____

2. I felt creative when _____

3. I wanted to _____

4. In my household, creativity was _____

5. I wished that I had _____

3. There are many things we *could* do if we were willing. Fill in the following sentence with an action you could take. They need not be serious. Write quickly, and see if what you uncover surprises you:

1. I could _____

2. I could _____

3. I could _____

4. I could _____

5. I could _____

6. I could _____

7. I could _____

8. I could _____

9. I could _____

10. I could _____

Name your next right action. Now take it.

4. So often, we see age as a barrier to our dreams. "It's too late" is a favored excuse. But is it ever really too late? We often assume that we are too old—or too young—for creative adventuring. But this is never the case. We are simply using our age, whatever age we are, as an excuse to deny ourselves joyful expansion.

Fill in the following sentence:

1. If it weren't too late, I would _____

2. If it weren't too late, I would _____

3. If it weren't too late, I would _____

4. If it weren't too late, I would _____

5. If it weren't too late, I would _____

6. If it weren't too late, I would _____

7. If it weren't too late, I would _____

8. If it weren't too late, I would _____

9. If it weren't too late, I would _____

10. If it weren't too late, I would _____

5. Take pen in hand and recall a time when your plans shifted and you went along with the change. Recall your pride in your own flexibility. Remind yourself that the

Higher Power is supportive whenever you are able to re-linquish control.

6. Age is a matter of appetite for life and attitude about our current life. Focused on the wonder of the world around us, our age becomes irrelevant. Take a twenty-minute walk, focusing on the beauty you find. Feel your age slip away as you take a childlike interest and pleasure in your environment.

7. Fill in the following sentence twenty-five times:

   1. I love . . . _____

   2. I love . . . _____

   3. I love . . . _____

   4. I love . . . _____

   5. I love . . . _____

Deceptively simple, this exercise trains us in small joys. Look at your list. What "love" can you give yourself today, right now? The depth of the satisfaction we get from a small but well-chosen treat may surprise us.

Now choose one "love" from your list. Give it to yourself.

THE PROSPERITY PLAN

As the course draws to a close, you will look at your resources of time, energy, talent, creativity, and money, and decide how you want to spend your assets. How you spend your time is how you spend your life—and how you spend your money can and should reflect your true values, your most prosperous vision for yourself. You have probably heard the saying, "Man makes plans and God laughs," but this does not mean "don't make plans." I interpret this to mean plan—and then be open to your plan being improved upon—by you, by God, by your neighbor. Be flexible and forward-thinking. True financial and spiritual prosperity are yours.

CREATING A PROSPERITY PLAN

In Counting, you have now come to know your spending patterns. Your habits have become familiar to you, and you have probably tweaked your behaviors so that your actions better reflect your values. In creating a Prosperity Plan, you now make decisions and set goals that will adjust the course of your spending on a daily basis and, ultimately, the course of your life.

The most important part of your Prosperity Plan is creating a plan for saving money. As long as you are earning more than you are spending, you are allowing yourself a future of prosperity as well. When we continuously live just beyond our means, we set ourselves up for future financial woes. Overspending, even by a tiny amount, puts us into debt, robbing ourselves of future freedoms. Once we have started the slippery habit of debting "just a little," it is a short distance to feelings of failure, of "what's the use," and then charging the new pair of shoes that we didn't really need—and can't afford. When we debt, we rob ourselves of our hopes. We take from ourselves both financially and spiritually.

In creating a Prosperity Plan, we must begin by charting the expenses we know we have: rent, food, entertainment—and then looking at how much we spend where. The Counting work we have been doing should give us a good idea of where our money is going. Then we need to consider each of these expenditures and decide whether they are fulfilling our needs in the best way possible or whether we need to consider making a change—ideally, a change that will allow us to reduce our expenses. For example, if we spend $50 a week on buying lunch we don't really like at the deli, but could actually make our lunch for $30 a week and put $20 in savings, this is an adjustment worth making.

"Listening is a form of accepting."
—STELLA TERRILL MANN

The idea of creating a Prosperity Plan is to *plan* where we will spend our money. We may have a vague plan to not spend any money, but this is unrealistic. Money is to be spent. And paying ourselves, by investing in our savings account, is a good way to spend it.

VOLUNTEERISM

When we have a sense of God's abundance and benevolence, we want to share it with others. As Chuck Chamberlain, a well-known early AA member in California, says, "We reach the point where our work is helping God's kids get done what they need to get done." So money for services rendered becomes sort of beside the point— which isn't to say that we don't bill for our services, because we do. But we often go an extra mile.

Right now, in Los Alamos, New Mexico, there is a wildfire. My home in Santa Fe smells of smoke, and the neighbors are warning one another to have a bag packed in the event of a quick escape. I called my friend Elberta, who lives about twenty miles north on a horse farm.

"We're rescuing horses," Elberta says. She is sending her workers out, free of charge, to save the horses near the fire and bring them back to her farm to safety. "We have gotten fifteen here so far." Elberta is acting out of nothing but her expansive heart. She asks for nothing in return. "I just hope we can save them all," she says.

All of us have ways that we can volunteer our time and talents. Volunteerism does not require money. It requires only generosity of energy and effort. And the return is often much larger than the investment. We are rewarded with gratitude and a sense of accomplishment.

My phone rang. It was a woman in Santa Fe whom I'd met years before, wanting to reconnect. Happy to hear from her, I scheduled a lunch.

"So we'll meet at one at Luminaria," Charlie Romney-Brown confirmed the plan.

"Where is Luminaria?" I asked.

"It's at the Inn of Loretto. East Alameda and Old Santa Fe Trail. I'm a blonde, and I think I'll remember you from seeing you at the Smithsonian. Could it be fifteen years ago?"

And so, at twelve thirty, I set off to find the Inn of Loretto. I knew to take Guadalupe to West Alameda, which would become East Alameda and intersect with Old Santa Fe Trail. I was meeting

Charlie Romney-Brown for a "getting to know you" lunch prior to my speaking at Women's Voices, as her pet project is named. She is a mover and shaker, a confirmed political activist, a true feminist who taught women's studies at Georgetown University, my alma mater.

The Inn of Loretto loomed suddenly into view. I gave my car to the valet, and he instructed me to take the long hallway to the left to Luminaria.

"I'm meeting Charlie Romney-Brown," I told the maître d'.

"Why, yes, she's here already," he replied. He showed me to a corner booth where a classically beautiful blonde was waiting.

"Hello," I greeted her. "I'm Julia."

"Yes, and I'm Charlie. It's good of you to come out."

"You're dressed to match our decor," I remarked. The walls were pewter toned, and so was her silk blouse.

"Yes, I guess I am." Charlie laughed. She leaned forward across the table. "Do you have a set speech you will be giving?" she asked.

"No," I said, "I'm afraid I'm a member of the 'pray and then open your mouth' club."

"I think that's the best."

Women's Voices, a charity and leadership organization, began during Charlie's years in Washington, D.C., where it was known as Defining Destiny. What started with seven women mushroomed to more than five hundred, hosting such speakers as Hillary Rodham Clinton and Gail Sheehy. I am pleased to have been chosen to join this company. Charlie herself could be a speaker. A published poet, she is also the author of a soon-to-be-published book on Mormon history and polygamy. Raised in a Mormon family, she entered an arranged marriage when she was eighteen. She left that marriage while in her early twenties and launched a lifelong career as a feminist and activist.

She quotes Margaret Mead: "Never doubt that a small group of

"I am enough."
—UNKNOWN

thoughtful, committed citizens can change the world. Indeed, it is the only thing that ever has." Women's Voices in Santa Fe also began with a cluster of women, and has grown now to more than two hundred fifty members.

Here is a woman who had a full-time job as a professor, who wrote poetry and books, but found the time to found and run an organization to empower women during a time when many doors were still closed to them. It is no surprise that Charlie has influenced—and inspired—many.

"One may not reach the dawn save by the path of the night."
—Kahlil Gibran

The prosperous heart is committed. It believes that it can make a difference. The prosperous heart focuses on what it *can* do, not on the odds stacked against it.

But few people are in the position that Charlie is in. Often, people who feel pinched financially believe that volunteering is only for the wealthy or retired. This is not true. All of us can volunteer in some small way. Sara, a single working mom, wanted to volunteer at her son's school, but felt shut out, as she couldn't make daytime PTA meetings, volunteer in the school library, or join her son and his classmates on field trips. Taking unpaid time off from work wasn't an option—it was hard enough making ends meet. But she was determined to help, and eventually found other ways to volunteer that didn't include daytime commitments. She began making fund-raising phone calls for her son's school during her lunch break, and editing the monthly newsletter in the evenings. As she saw the school's reserve fund and newsletter's circulation grow, she felt a deep sense of satisfaction in her ability to contribute.

Whether we give our time to a soup kitchen or an after-school program, or are the visionary behind a nonprofit organization, when we volunteer our time and energy for a cause we believe in, we experience the meaning of true prosperity.

VALUABLE GIFTS

In twelve-step jargon, "You have to give it away to keep it." The "it" you give away is usually spiritual in nature. No matter how much money you have, there are always gifts you can give that are more valuable than money.

"Money is a tool," says Kate, a visionary businesswoman who pours the benefits of her success into college funds for her large extended family. "And you can't convince me there is anything more important than education."

An avid gardener and inspired cook, Kate shares her talents freely with her friends and family. "When my husband and I started to make money, the first thing we did was expand the kitchen into a place where all of the kids could join in the cooking." Today, the now grown-up kids still return to that kitchen, nourished by Kate's generous spirit as much as her delectable creations.

"I grew up in this kitchen," her niece Leah says. Now in art school, she has her aunt to thank for her education—and her values. "Aunt Kate taught me how to cook—and how to dream. She taught all of us. She can see our talents before they really develop. It's like she's clairvoyant or something."

It is no coincidence that in her professional life, Kate's vocation is to "see" projects before they fully exist. Reading potential as much as anything else, Kate, a movie studio executive, is responsible for the successes of many a writer, actor, and director. Deflecting attention from herself when her more effusive colleagues and relatives dedicate triumph after triumph to her, Kate keeps her laser focus strongly fixed on the needs and talents of each person she encourages. Able in very few words to offer true and individual clarity, she is the quiet strength behind a lucky group of people.

"We know we are blessed," says her nephew Gerard. "Kate's awesome."

"Money is a singular thing. It ranks with love as man's greatest source of joy, and with death as his greatest source of anxiety."
—JOHN KENNETH GALBRAITH

Indeed. She is not only teaching the people around her to bet on themselves, but she is also teaching them how to bet on others. "I became a teacher because Aunt Kate treated me with so much respect," says Gerard. "By believing in me, she gave me a responsibility—and I wanted to live up to it. Now I want to help others in the same way. I can't wait until the day I can start a scholarship fund in her name. Passing on education—and opportunities for education—is my life's work."

Kate has gifted her family with opportunities for education—and an education in gifting what we can. Helping others accomplish their goals and meet their potential can be done in other ways as well.

When Marcia's son asked to audition for a play at the local community theater, she encouraged him to do so. His friends were auditioning as well, and it seemed like a good summer project for him. She noted that several of his friends, if cast, would likely have a hard time getting to and from rehearsals. They had single or working parents, and public transportation was scarce in the area. Suspecting they would all be cast, and knowing what the opportunity would mean to them all, Marcia formulated a plan, and auditioned for the play herself.

When they all were given roles, Marcia offered to be the chauffeur, saying even before the boys could raise the question that she would drive them all to and from rehearsals. Happy to be involved, and happier still that the talented boys would be able to participate in the play, Marcia gave them all the gift of the experience. Understanding the value of the opportunity, she allowed it to happen for all of them. She also surprised herself. She hadn't performed in a play since high school, and was overjoyed at her reconnection with the stage. "I think I've still got it," she said with a laugh. Indeed. Marcia does have "it"—like Kate, "it" is a spirit that enlarges those around her.

ASKING FOR GUIDANCE

Praying for knowledge of God's will for us and the power to carry it out is simple but radical. We are sometimes led in new directions, down avenues we've scarcely imagined. When Emma, my collaborator, found a new writing partner, I felt jealous and displaced. Wanting to be glad for her, I took to my knees, asking for the grace to be generous. I prayed for knowledge of God's will for me and the power to carry it out. What came to me was the radical idea to leave New York and go to Santa Fe. Before New York, I had lived in New Mexico for ten years, and its beauty still called to me. My heart longed for sagebrush and piñon, for magpies and eagles. Nature always gave me a sense of abundance. With enough nature, I just might manage not to feel slighted. I began planning my move, counting money, hiring movers in Santa Fe. As my heart filled up with a sense of adventure, it stopped focusing on loss. I was experiencing an answered prayer.

Spiritual writer Sophy Burnham has remarked that many times we feel our prayers have gone unanswered because the answers we receive are so different from what we expect. Praying about my jealousy, I was answered with, "Go to Santa Fe." It was an answer that filled up my impoverished heart. My ego was shattered by Emma's new collaboration, but my answered prayer ignored my wounded ego. With a full heart, who has time for petty grievances? Not I, I found to my delight. Promised a grand adventure, my heart became generous. I was able to bow gracefully out of center stage. After all, Emma and I had enjoyed ten years of collaboration. Why be greedy? Move on. When I picked up the cue that was offered to me, I was able to be happy for Emma and Tyler. I was able to hear them when they told me of their admiration for me, help them when they asked for my advice, feel their deep respect for what I had to offer.

Santa Fe seemed to come out of left field, but it also made per-

"Real prosperity benefits not only the one receiving, but all mankind as well."
—Margaret Ponders

fect sense. Try as I might, I didn't find much beauty in the urban land-scape of New York. Emma, by contrast, spotted beauty everywhere in the city. I would catch fleeting glimpses of the flowers at a Korean market. Emma appreciated all of the passing storefronts. She loved shoe stores and bead stores, handbag stores and vintage clothing shops. Where I saw a jumble, she saw miraculous diversity.

For ten years I had lectured myself to find beauty in Manhattan's cornucopia. But when I made a list of things I loved, it stubbornly came up mountains, magpies, eagles, sagebrush, piñon—the sights and sounds of New Mexico. Whenever any of my friends spoke to me of the Southwest, I would get a stinging pang. "Let's talk about something else," I would say, and my friends would obligingly change the subject. Years after leaving New Mexico, I still experienced homesickness for its beauty. The thought that I could go back never crossed my mind. After all, I had experienced two catastrophic breakdowns in Taos, where medical help was scanty. And then it came to me: Santa Fe, not Taos. I would not so much be going back as going forward to a new adventure. I would regain the beauty, yet be in a city. I could have the best of both worlds. I just needed to take a chance. I asked for guidance, and listened for what I heard.

I could be adventuresome, I realized. The risk to be taken could be put in God's hands. "It will all be okay," I found myself thinking. I would miss Emma keenly, but our paths seemed destined to sep-arate. For the past year she had often flown to Chicago to work with Tyler. In her absence, I had been on my own, and I found that I did well. Our work could—and does—continue long-distance. I found myself feeling a sense of divine accompaniment as I took steps toward my new life. I would venture to Santa Fe accompanied by God. Emma would remain in New York, with God as her co-pilot there.

Having decided to make the move, I ran into support at every turn. It seemed that everyone I told had a good friend in Santa Fe,

"Perhaps one of the most startling secrets about prosperity is the Truth that the door lies right within yourself."

—REBECCA CLARK

someone I would love to meet. I began jotting down names and numbers. If even half of them panned out, I would be well provided for. My friend Jane Cecil took great delight in how everything was unfolding. To her, it seemed clear that I was following God's will.

It was good to receive Jane's reassurances. She so often held the longer view. Her forty years on the spiritual path had taught her optimism. She had over and over again witnessed difficult events working out. "Are you taken care of today?" Jane would ask.

When I said yes, Jane would ask next, "What makes you think you won't be taken care of tomorrow?" In Jane's view we always have a choice between fear and faith. If we elect to be fearful, that's our choice. Wouldn't it be saner to elect to have faith? Jane thought so.

Judy Collins was another optimistic friend. "I think it's fabulous," she declared. Born and raised in Denver, she still experienced the call of the West, although she has lived in New York all of her adult life. "I still think of going back," she admitted—a surprise to me, as she seemed so very at home in New York. She cheered me on.

Now at home in Santa Fe, I see in hindsight how I was indeed guided at every turn. Everything did fall into place. I was not alone at any point in the transition. Settled in, I have found friends easily. I enjoy the slower pace. I love the mountains and am fascinated by their changing faces as the sun moves through the day. Now it is so obvious. Of *course* I was right to have faith, and to act on my guidance.

"I identify myself with abundance, health and happiness. I associate myself with the vast All. I identify myself with everything necessary to make my life complete."
—ERNEST HOLMES

Last night was Wednesday night, and I cooked for my friends. We had roast chicken with risotto, spinach salad, fruit salad, candied carrots, fresh sliced beets, and, for dessert, cherry pie and sour cream raisin pie, an old family recipe.

"Everything is delicious!" exclaimed Rick. "I think I'm going to have seconds." Soon the chicken was down to bare bones. The candied carrots and beets were gobbled up. Extra helpings of risotto were scooped onto crowded plates. Conversation dipped to a low while people focused on their food.

"I'll need some help with cleanup," I told the group.

"Of course we'll help with cleanup!" Karma exclaimed. "You did all the cooking. I'd like to get the recipe for the raisin pie," he added. I myself had gotten the recipe from my sister Lorrie. She found it on a card in her recipe box and noted that the handwriting was our mother's. After seconds on dinner, people still had room for pie and ice cream, and seconds on that.

"Let's get at the dishes," Karma suggested.

"Yes, let's," echoed Michele. Soon the entire dinner party was in the kitchen, scraping, scrubbing, and stacking the plates into the dishwasher. Michele went to work wiping down counters. Karma attacked the stove. Before long, the kitchen was in better shape than it had been when I started cooking. Soon even the serving dishes were clean and stacked back in their proper places. I packed up care packages to go home with my guests. By eight thirty, they were putting on their coats and heading out the door.

Praying for guidance, we listen to the hunches that come to us. Acting on our guidance, we receive more guidance. We gradually come to trust the still, small voice within us. We become spontaneous rather than fearful. We trust God and we trust ourselves.

Prosperity point: take pen in hand and ask a question on which you need guidance. Listen for what you "hear" and write it down. All of us have access to a larger and wiser self. Allow yourself to answer in the persona of a knowing "someone." You may turn to Obi-Wan Kenobi, a spiritual guide or even Glinda the Good Witch or a fairy godmother. Whomever you choose, trust the input you receive. It will often be simpler and more direct than you expect. The prosperous heart is open-minded. It experiences many things beyond the realm of the ordinary.

THE PROSPEROUS HEART

What makes us happy people? If it were money, that would be easy. But it is more complex than that. Happiness—true spiritual prosperity—is an attitude, a choice we make in every moment. Seven-year-old Tegan, finding a quarter, might feel rich, while another, at the height of his fortune, may well feel poor. Stripped of the convenient distraction of stress over money—how we don't have enough, didn't have enough, one day might not have enough—we are complete. Sometimes vulnerable, sometimes unsure, sometimes elated, sometimes bored, inspired, confused, excited—this is the human experience—but always ourselves. And it is enough.

When you slip backward and find yourself reverting to old spending habits—and you will—do not be discouraged. You can always go back to the basic tools, and you will always find your way back to clarity when you do. If you do find yourself slipping, ask yourself why. Is there something in your life that is upsetting you? Is something causing you fear or sadness? Are you narcotizing yourself by spending, knowing that the act of spending can numb your feelings—like any other addictive behavior—and the ensuing worry that overspending causes can distract you from your true feelings and desires? Whether you reach for a cigarette, a drink, or a credit card in times of stress, it's all the same.

The answer to what ails you is not as simple as just "having more money." As Richard Rodgers, the composer/producer, said, "If it can be solved with money, it's not really a problem." Because we are so accustomed to worrying about money, we use this familiar worry as a block to our true feelings and desires. We need not pretend that we exist in a world without money, that we are above money, that we don't care about money. But money *is* a tool, and it is a tool we can use to better our lives. We can reassess. We can begin anew, resolving to Count again. We can take a Time-Out. We can reevaluate our spending plan to reflect changes that come to us. The trick is to rally, to assume that any financial worry has something else underneath it, and to be willing to look.

As Einstein remarked, "In the midst of adversity lies opportunity." Believing this, we can face difficult times with curiosity. "What is God up to here?" we ask. The answer is often something that brings us happiness.

So often when we hear, "It will happen when it's meant to happen," whether in relation to money, recognition, love—we feel frustrated by the apparent callousness of that remark. I would say this to you: be open to surprise. Financial recovery is a continual challenge for many people, but the reward is well worth it. As we "right" ourselves every day by maintaining our own financial and spiritual clarity, we right ourselves with the world as well. Be alert to support from all quarters. Help and happiness may come from where you least expect it. You are meant to flourish. Live long and prosper.

WEEK TWELVE CHECK-IN

Morning Pages: Did you do them this week? How many days?

Counting: Did you count this week? What did you learn?

Abstinence: Did you abstain from debting this week? If you did debt, what was it for? How did you feel?

Walking: Did you walk this week? What insights did you have?

Time-Out: Did you take your Time-Outs? What did you learn?

Prosperity Points

1. Look back at your Counting and assess where your money goes by filling in the following chart:

SPENDING CATEGORY	AMOUNT THIS WEEK
1. Food (groceries)	$41.89
2. Dining out	$161
3. Rent	$400 (¼ of month)
4. Entertainment	$0
5. Clothes	$0
6. Gifts	$24 (flowers for Patt H.)
7. Travel: subway/car	$34.77 (gas in car)
8. Pharmacy/drugstore purchases	$55.60 (refilled prescriptions)
9. Snacks/newsstand purchases	$32 (magazines)
10. Household bills (cable, Internet)	$54.11 (paid bills this week)

Now make a prosperity plan about how you could improve your spending. By planning where our money will go and allowing for expenses, we often end up having a little more left over than we expected.

PROSPERITY PLAN	
1. Food (groceries)	$60/week
2. Dining out	$60/week
3. Rent	$400 (¼ of month)

4. Entertainment	$25/week
5. Clothes	$30 (if needed)
6. Gifts	$30 (if needed)
7. Travel: subway/car	$34.77 (gas in car)
8. Pharmacy/drugstore purchases	$55.60 (refilled prescriptions)
9. Snacks/newsstand purchases	$10
10. Household bills (cable, Internet)	$50 to credit card

As we plan our money *before* we spend it, we can adjust accordingly. We can buy groceries so that we don't get caught snacking or buying fast food in a pinch. We can plan to go to the movies. Deciding where our money will go, we can plan to have enough for what we need, and even what we want.

2. Is there some arena to which you can commit your time and talents? Take pen in hand. Describe what your commitment would entail. What does it look like? Imagine the rewards—to you and to others—for your commitment.

3. Take pen in hand and write out one passionate belief that you could share. When you have finished, phone a friend and share what you have written. Allow your friend's faith to piggyback on your own. Sharing our deepest dreams and desires, we share true prosperity with others.

4. Complete the following phrase:

   1. I would like guidance about _____

   2. I would like guidance about _____

3. I would like guidance about _____

4. Iwould like guidance about _____

5. I would like guidance about _____

6. I would like guidance about _____

7. I would like guidance about _____

8. I would like guidance about _____

9. I would like guidance about _____

10. I would like guidance about _____

List three times when you trusted your intuition and it turned out to be accurate.
1. I bought the less expensive watch, which has held up for years.
2. I bought the more expensive computer, which has turned out to be a good investment.
   Etc.

Fill in the following sentence:

1. I could choose to have faith about _____

2. I could choose to have faith about _____

3. I could choose to have faith about _____

4. I could choose to have faith about _____

5. I could choose to have faith about _____

6. I could choose to have faith about _____

7. I could choose to have faith about _____

8. I could choose to have faith about _____

9. I could choose to have faith about _____

10. I could choose to have faith about _____

EPILOGUE:
STARTING OVER

Slipping is part of recovery. We miss a day of Counting, we spend unnecessarily, we lend money to the person we resolved we would avoid—these are natural human foibles. Living a prosperous life means living a day at a time. It means starting over each morning, forgiving ourselves and beginning anew when we make mistakes, picking ourselves up when we fall, keeping on track. If we do the work, and keep an ear cocked for the grace and guidance of God, we will reap the rewards.

There is a folktale that goes something like this: A man is seeking God, and as he begins his journey, he comes upon a wolf in the forest.

"Will you share your food with me?" the wolf asks the man.

"No," says the man, "I don't have time. I am seeking God, and I cannot be distracted."

The man continues on his way. As he crosses a river, a woman appears nearby.

"I'm lonely," says the woman. "Will you be my companion?"

"No," says the man, "I don't have time. I am seeking God, and I cannot be distracted."

The man continues on. He passes a tree, which whispers, "Please help free my roots. I can't drink enough water, and I am thirsty. Will you dig out the rock that blocks my nourishment?"

"No," says the man, "I don't have time. I am seeking God, and I cannot be distracted."

The man reaches the edge of the forest, and when he emerges, he finds nothing. Lost and alone, he collapses to the ground.

"Why have you forsaken me, God? Where are you? Why am I alone and lost, when all I have done is seek you?"

"I placed the wolf in your path to protect you," says God. "I put the woman on earth to be your soul mate. And the rock that blocked the roots of the tree was a treasure chest. But you ignored everything I tried to give to you."

Let us not ignore the gifts that are given to us.

Having a prosperous heart is a daily endeavor. We must begin anew every day, consciously, stubbornly, choosing faith. No matter what our circumstances, there *is* help available to us. We are not alone. We will receive guidance when we ask for it. The still, small voice will always speak when we listen for it.

I look out the window at the delicate birds on my feeders. A hummingbird hovers so close that I feel like I could almost touch it. I am entranced by its tiny body, its steadiness, its strength. "I am prosperity," it whispers.

I am happy here. The hummingbird is enough.

ACKNOWLEDGMENTS

Tyler Beattie, for his insight

Domenica Cameron-Scorsese, for her example

Sara Carder, for her faith

Sonia Choquette, for her vision

Joel Fotinos, for his inspiration

Linda Kahn, for her expertise

Rob and Martha Lively, for their generosity

Susan Raihofer, for her unflagging support

Discover Julia Cameron's Creative Kingdom

©Aloma

To order, call 1-800-788-6262 or visit our website at www.penguin.com

BOOKS IN *THE ARTIST'S WAY* SERIES

The Artist's Way
· ISBN   978-1-58542-147-3 (hardcover)
· ISBN   978-1-58542-146-6 (trade paper)
· ISBN   978-0-14-305825-0 (audio, CDs)

Walking in This World
ISBN   978-1-58542-261-6 (trade paper)

Finding Water
· ISBN   978-1-58542-463-4 (hardcover)
· ISBN   978-1-58542-777-2 (trade paper)

The Artist's Way Workbook
ISBN   978-1-58542-533-4 (trade paper)

The Artist's Way Morning Pages Journal
ISBN   978-0-87477-886-1 (trade paper)

The Complete Artist's Way
ISBN   978-1-58542-630-0 (hardcover)

The Artist's Way Every Day
ISBN   978-1-58542-747-5 (trade paper)

The Artist's Date Book
ISBN   978-0-87477-653-9 (trade paper)

Inspirations: Meditations from
The Artist's Way
ISBN   978-1-58542-102-2 (trade paper)

OTHER BOOKS ON CREATIVITY

The Right to Write
ISBN   978-1-58542-009-4 (trade paper)

The Sound of Paper
ISBN   978-1-58542-354-5 (trade paper)

The Writing Diet
ISBN   978-1-58542-698-0 (trade paper)

The Vein of Gold
ISBN   978-0-87477-879-3 (trade paper)

How to Avoid Making Art (or Anything Else You Enjoy)
ISBN   978-1-58542-438-2 (trade paper)

The Writer's Life: Insights from The Right to Write
ISBN   978-1-58542-103-9 (trade paper)

Supplies: A Troubleshooting Guide for Creative Difficulties
ISBN   978-1-58542-212-8

The Creative Life: True Tales of Inspiration
ISBN   978-1-58542-824-3

PRAYER BOOKS

Answered Prayers
ISBN   978-1-58542-351-4 (trade paper)

Heart Steps
ISBN   978-0-87477-899-1 (trade paper)

Blessings
ISBN   978-0-87477-906-6 (trade paper)

Transitions
ISBN   978-0-87477-995-0 (trade paper)

Prayers to the Great Creator
· ISBN   978-1-58542-682-9 (hardcover)
· ISBN   978-1-58542-778-9 (trade paper)

BOOKS ON SPIRITUALITY

Faith and Will
ISBN   978-1-58542-714-7 (hardcover)

Prayers from a Nonbeliever
ISBN   978-1-58542-213-5 (hardcover)

Letters to a Young Artist
ISBN   978-1-58542-409-2 (hardcover)

God Is No Laughing Matter
ISBN   978-1-58542-128-2 (trade paper)

MEMOIR

Floor Sample: A Creative Memoir
· ISBN   978-1-58542-494-8 (hardcover)
· ISBN   978-158542-557-0 (trade paper)

Watch Julia Cameron on Tarcher Talks @ www.penguin.com/tarchertalks

GIVE THE GIFT OF
CREATIVE INSPIRATION

Two *Artist's Way* gift sets are now available to mark the 20th anniversary of this international bestseller.

A $75 value, for just $59

978-1-58542-927-1
The Artist's Way: Creative Kingdom Collection is a gorgeous box set that contains Julia Cameron's most essential tools—*The Artist's Way*, *The Artist's Way Workbook*, *The Artist's Way Morning Pages Journal*, and the *Artist's Way* audiobook. The *Kingdom Collection* offers everything an aspiring writer or artists need to fully experience Cameron's life-changing creativity program.

978-1-58542-928-8 · $29.95
The Artist's Way Starter Kit includes Cameron's two most important tools—*The Artist's Way* and *The Artist's Way Morning Pages Journal*—attractively shrink-wrapped together with a belly band. This *Starter Kit* is the perfect entry point for those who want to start unblocking their creativity!

*For more information, visit www.JuliaCameronLive.com
or www.tarcherbooks.com/juliacameron.*

THE PROSPEROUS HEART

Also by Julia Cameron

BOOKS ON SPIRITUALITY

Prayers from a Nonbeliever

Letters to a Young Artist

God Is No Laughing Matter

God Is Dog Spelled Backwards
(illustrated by Elizabeth Cameron)

Faith and Will

MEMOIR

Floor Sample: A Creative Memoir

FICTION

Mozart's Ghost

Popcorn: Hollywood Stories

The Dark Room

PLAYS

Public Lives

The Animal in the Trees

Four Roses

Love in the DMZ

Avalon (a musical)

The Medium at Large (a musical)

Magellan (a musical)

POETRY

Prayers for the Little Ones

Prayers for the Nature Spirits

The Quiet Animal

This Earth (also an album with Tim Wheater)

FEATURE FILM
(as writer-director) *God's Will*